The Final Swipe

**HEAL YOUR HEART,
FIND YOUR PERSON,
AND END THE DATING
SEARCH FOR GOOD**

Nikki Novo

The Final Swipe:
Heal Your Heart, Find Your Person and End the Dating Search for Good

Copyright © 2018 by Nikki Novo
First edition
ISBN: 978-0-9908042-1-5

Book Design by Laura Wrubleski
Edited by Alicia Palma-Espinoza and Kelsey Straight
Creative Direction by Giselle Macias
Publishing Support by The Self Publishing Agency

Nikki Novo Writes LLC
www.nikkinovo.com

For our lucky number three, Ethan.
Thank you for the courage you placed inside of me.
I love you, eternally.

Contents

Introduction

Remember when we thought our dating experience would play out just like a romantic comedy?

The quirky, chronically single girl who loves her dog meets a guy at jury duty, who she hates at first for his good looks and suave moves. Forced to get to know him, she discovers that he's actually a mythical creature who sees past her insecurities and doubts. He falls in love with her and proves it's safe to fall for him, too— during a scene at the airport. They live happily ever after. The end.

I can't tell you how many times I've dreamt of being seated next to my future husband on a flight from Miami to Los Angeles; I would imagine an emerging screenwriter with Midwestern values who experienced some early career success, but hadn't found someone to share it with. Of course, he wanted to settle down one day, get married, and have kids, but he was struggling in the dating scene. There were no good girls out there anymore. Enter: Me.

Perhaps surprisingly, this never happened to me. No way! It never happened to you either? I guess that's why you picked up this book. And why I'm the one writing this book. Because I totally get you.

For a long time, you thought it would eventually just happen. You're a good person. You take care of yourself. You try your best to stay positive. You have plenty of friends. You're good at what you do. Dammit, you even volunteer and give back to your community. Yet for some reason, the universe refuses to help a sister out!

Instead, you've encountered a ton of heartbreak, disappointment, embarrassment, and anxiety—to the point that you think, *Maybe this isn't going to happen for me?*

I am here to tell you it is. Will it happen on a five-hour flight? The chances are a bit slim. But I wholeheartedly believe that if you do the inner work you are being called to do, you will find that partner.

In my practice as an intuitive dating coach, I'm constantly asked about the future. So many people ask because, as individuals, we're nervous, impatient, and *not* okay with surrendering control. But we also ask this question because there's a part of us that believes in fate.

Logically, we understand that by putting our minds to something, we can make it happen. We can literally will it into being. But dating feels different. Why? Because there's someone else involved. We know we can't manifest our way into making someone fall in love with us, which is why we can't help but think, *Maybe a romantic partner is not in the cards for me.*

Here's why that thought is wrong. The desires placed in our hearts are there to be realized; when we long for something, it's because we're capable of bringing it into our lives. We don't dream of things that are not a possibility for us.

In fact, dreaming about it is the first step to making it happen. It's the conception of a possibility. That possibility is our fate. The thing is, we completely get in the way of our fate.

This book was created with the intention of getting you back on the path of your fate. As you read these pages, you will undo the blocks and heal the past. You will become clear on what you want in a partnership—and you will learn to date in a way that feels right, like you're moving in the right direction.

We often look at dating as a means to an end—this torturous process we endure to find true love. With that attitude, no wonder it's so hard for us to see results!

Can we really blame ourselves for dating this way? After all, our society shames us for failing. If you date long enough, every experience ends up a failure, so our instinct is either to make the wrong thing work out, or quit before things get worse.

What we're doing is leading with fear rather than love. All the choices we make about dating are fear-based choices. We choose to be incredibly active on the dating apps for fear of ending up alone. We decide not to put ourselves out there for fear of being rejected. We decide not to over-text someone for fear of losing control.

What if for a change we could look for love by leading with love? That's what this book is about.

I have this crazy idea about dating. I believe it is a sacred time in our life that should be seen with reverence and joy. I believe that dating is one of the most important seasons of a woman's life. Not only is it an opportunity for tremendous spiritual growth, but it is a pivotal time in the weaving of our future.

Who we pick as life partners influences all areas of our lives, especially for those of us who want the whole shebang—marriage, career, children, and so on. This person impacts our career, our family, our finances, where we live, and so many other choices.

I don't mean to overwhelm you, but your life partner is a big deal! For this reason, I want you to approach this with a pure heart. This book is our way of sorting through your baggage. I want you to toss out what you don't need and incorporate more of what you do, because when you start from a place of clarity and worth, the results will exceed your wildest dreams. I know this, because I was exactly where you are. The day I decided (i.e. was forced) to do the work was the same day my luck completely turned around.

My search for love started really young. Actually, it was more of a search for self than love. At 20-years-old, I was engaged to my high school sweetheart. I wasn't able to legally drink alcohol at my engagement party, but I was totally allowed to make this huge life decision of marriage. I was looking to get married for all the wrong reasons. I had the kind of upbringing that made me believe I could either move out of my house in a white dress or a casket. A wedding seemed like the better option.

At the time, I was looking for independence, but I thought the only way there was by having a man take care of me. When I met my high school sweetheart, I was subconsciously looking for my parents to approve of my partner. I wanted someone who could support me financially and get me out of my hometown.

The universe supplied me with just that. He was a kind, Cuban-American boy who happened to be a star baseball player. A few years into our relationship, he signed a lucrative contract to play professional baseball. He ultimately fit all my requirements. There was only one problem: I wasn't in love. How could I love him? I didn't even know how to love myself, nevermind another person.

Two months before our scheduled, Big Fat Cuban wedding, I found myself in New York City visiting a girlfriend. I remember standing in Rockefeller Center watching the ice skaters go by, in one of the loudest cities on Earth, and hearing a whisper. My intuition was trying to get my attention to tell me that I was on the wrong path. It told me I was meant for something more.

I came home a few days later and called the whole thing off: the wedding, the relationship, the fake life. I mourned for about two weeks, before realizing that I had my entire life in front of me. I always wanted to work in the film industry, so I decided to pack my car and move across the country to Los Angeles.

Girl, we can run, but we cannot hide from our baggage. I was in L.A. to further my career, but deep down, I was trying to find myself. Unfortunately, my way of finding myself was through men and dating. I didn't know this at the time, but looking for love to feel loved isn't really a great idea. Let's just say the universe taught me a lot of lessons through my dating life, lessons it wants to teach us all.

With each and every guy I dated—and let's be honest, some I just slept with—I found light and shadows. I found my free-spirited nature, smarts, wounds, dreams, and fears—all through this giant mirror called dating.

Dating is a mirror. One that can be harsh. Our insecurities become so loud during this process; it feels unbearable, but then we remember what we want. Our souls remind us that a romantic partnership is part of the plan, and against our better judgment, we try again.

Towards the end of my time in California, I was trying to make one relationship into something it wasn't. When things didn't go my way, I decided to cement my roots back to Miami. Thinking myself ready to settle down, I moved back to my hometown. Within the first month of being home, my mom dragged me to church, probably praying for the demons of La Vida Loca to leave my body. I didn't mind; I figured the guy in the sky could help me out with this one love situation I couldn't quite crack.

I prayed for a boyfriend who'd ultimately turn into my husband. Someone who'd love me for me, bring out my best self, and save me from the anxiety of being single. It didn't take long for my prayers to be answered. I was quite impressed by this God person. *Thank you, God,* I thought. *I'll be sure to do business with you again soon.*

Sweet, this universal source ended up coming through—it sent me a boyfriend! He was even wrapped in a perfect bow: creative, educated, sexy, from a good family, had a job… Check, check, check!

We instantly fell in love, like two magnets finding their other halves. Our relationship was a Nicholas Sparks novel in the making. In fact, it was exactly how I envisioned it: romantic, passionate, and poetic, with sprinkles of dedicated song lyrics—but before you close this book and demand a refund, know this relationship is only the beginning of my story.

Just a few months into our relationship, I could feel this strong sensation in my stomach, suggesting that our love would fall apart one day soon. Based on the current state of our relationship, I had nothing to worry about, but I could feel it deep inside. I even phoned friends in healthy, long-lasting relationships and asked if they, too, felt this sensation. Perhaps feeling so terrified of losing someone was a sign of true love, yet no one could relate to my gut feeling.

A year and a half later, we broke up, and I, like many women who try to make things into what they're not, found myself completely off guard. The relationship, which I thought was a gift from God, had crumbled.

I'm not one for failure. I had already made the decision to make a living as a "creative," so the one sensible thing I could do by my family and society's standard was lock down a relationship with a clear path to marriage. Plus, a steady romantic relationship was an item on my checklist, which I so desperately wanted to check off. It was as if I couldn't move forward and see the light, until I had checked that box. Only then would I be happy and confident enough to move forward with my life.

So yeah, while this breakup was one big blow to the ego, I'm stubborn. This "failure" only made me more determined to conquer true love, and so my journey began.

My newly ignited determination was a great trait to have on my side, but there was one problem: If I didn't know what true love was, how would I ever find it? In truth, I didn't find love for a long time, but I managed to take some surface steps anyway. I lived my journey and started to realize that I did have a kind of strategy. I wasn't aware of it, but there was some kind of energy definitively guiding me along the path of love. My strategy was to find out what love *wasn't*—then I'd go from there.

At the time, I thought a relationship would verify my existence, subsequently making me happy. Society was telling me that I did not count unless I was part of a pair. Plus, having someone by my side who loved me unconditionally seemed the perfect Band-Aid to cover up my deepest insecurities. Basically, I felt that relationships were a universal vote of confidence.

Likewise, the idea of a committed relationship sounded safe. Dating, on the other hand, was one big emotional roller coaster. *Does he like me? Did I text the right thing? His arm is on my lap—does that mean anything?* I liked being in control of my emotions, and while dating didn't always allow for such control, the fear of being alone was worse. What was a recently dumped, broken-hearted girl searching for a relationship to do? Date like it was her job, and this became my personal mission.

Unfortunately, I was a hot mess. I jumped from guy to guy, dating them only until we reached that point where I became vulnerable, or else got the heck out to save myself from getting hurt. You know, that point before you've shown your true colors. After all, on the outside I seemed put together; I was kind, smart, driven, but anyone who got too close could tell that I was imperfect.

I realized then how much fear I held inside of me: Fear of being rejected. Fear of not being enough. Fear of being alone. And most of all: Fear of having to accept love. Because the last thing you want when you don't feel worthy is to be stuck in a position where you have to accept love. Succumbing to love only means you might lose it one day. Just imagine what that can do to your self-esteem.

Fear is never a good enough reason to refrain from doing something. A part of me knew that I could not give up on true love. I knew it was out there. I knew it wasn't how it looks in the movies. But I did know it was close.

So I worked through my pain, meaning I continued to date. On the outside, it may have seemed as if I were searching for a life partner, but really I was just going through the motions. I was pretty sad at the time; distracting myself with a slew of eligible bachelors was my way of avoiding internal chaos.

I kept my composure together on the outside (who am I kidding, I only *thought* I was keeping my composure together; everyone knows a hot mess when they see one)! Inside, I had some inner work to do. Along the way, I received spiritual guidance and began to understand that like attracts like. I became aware that we attract people who reflect our inner beliefs. Considering that my inner beliefs were out-of-whack, it was no surprise that the relationships I attracted neither completed nor saved me, as I hoped they would.

Although I'd met plenty of great guys on my dating marathon, none of them felt right. It became obvious that I had to make a change. Many people reach a point in their dating careers—when nothing seems to fit—and feel the need to move across the country, or consider changing their gender preference. But I had this eerie feeling that the solution to my so-called problem was a lot closer. Even if I ran away to another state, I knew my baggage would follow.

So I hit a crossroad. One path was that of settling for a mediocre life, a mediocre relationship, a mediocre job … a mediocre self. The other path meant looking myself in the face and saying, *The answers are inside of you, and you know that.*

I didn't stop dating to embark on an eat-pray-love trip, or anything glamorous like that. Instead, I got to work. I read every personal-development book that drew my attention—even the ones with scary titles that turn your Amazon recommendations into a very sad list.

I tried different healing modalities; everything from hypnosis and Reiki to Theta Healing and plain 'ole prayer. I attended seminars, lectures, and hippie drum circles, dabbling in things I loved like yoga, traveling, writing and drinking wine with friends.

Basically, I would try anything that brought me happiness, and following this happiness eventually led me to understand that I was on a totally different mission than I thought. My mission was to feel complete on my own, regardless of my relationship status.

Just to make things clear, feeling whole wasn't going to substitute my desire for a life partner. I wanted both. I wanted to feel good about myself, so that I could meet someone who had the same level of self-worth. In order to meet someone that self-aware, I understood the search would need to start inside of me.

Returning to the wholeness I was born with is still a daily practice for me, but throughout my journey, I reached a place of transformation where I felt complete. My new place of functioning was sustainable, and I was able to attract the kind of life partner that I'd always deserved. Before doing all this soul-seeking work, I used to say that I would never meet anyone in my hometown. I believed I'd never meet anyone through my current friendships—after all, I was much more *evolved* than everyone, you know?

Guess what? I met my husband at my best friend's engagement party. This was my best friend from grade school! I knew every single one of her friends and family members. Plus, she was dating her fiancé long enough that I knew all of his friends, as well. The rest is history.

I am so grateful to my former self for doing the work. As the years have gone by, I watch other relationships struggle. I see friends lose who they are because they committed to the wrong person. I see marriages fall apart because they were built on poor soil. I see people who are totally bored. I truly believe that, as women, we build our future starting in the dating phase. It is the seed that will sprout in all areas of our future lives.

I see dating as sacred work. We often wonder about our purpose because we want to make an impact; we fail to realize the holiness of our daily lives, and dating is no exception. The union you create as a result of this process is part of your purpose. This is one of your holy missions. Do not ignore your intuition and settle for the first thing. Feel your way through it. Trust, believe, enjoy, for this moment is just one thread in the web of your magnificent life.

AUTHOR'S NOTE

In this book, I speak to a "she" looking for a "he," but please know that the wisdom shared within knows no gender. Love is love, indeed.

I use the words God, the universe, the divine, source, and spirit interchangeably. There's no word grand enough to explain it, so I use as many words as possible.

Lastly, open your heart to the message and healing, girl. It won't hurt as much as you think. I promise.

Step One:
KNOW YOURSELF

On the outside, I was actively looking for love; on the inside, I was hurt, disillusioned, and downright tired. Still, I continued to take all the steps: putting myself out there, saying yes to dates, leaving my couch, and anything else that the dating book written by the guy with the frosted tips told me to do.

Nonetheless, every relationship was short-lived and ended in either disappointment, rejection, or the feeling that I'd just dodged a bullet. I was meeting a lot of great guys—even the ones with drug problems were ultimately good people—but the right man just wouldn't show up. When I say right, I don't mean Mr. Right, because he was an urban legend invented to feed our perfectionist tendencies. What I mean is the right person for me. The man who was going to love me enough to stick around, despite my imperfections—the man who would allow me to love him back, too. Or was that too much to ask?

As I began to look at my friends, who were coupled up and on their way to decorated ring fingers, I couldn't help but feel there was something wrong with me. On the days I felt good about myself, I thought there must be something wrong with all the men in the world! I tried to make some of them work. There was one who made me listen to his voicemail message of another women asking him to hang out. He wanted to make sure that I knew he was passing up some hot booty, because he liked me so much. Sweet, right?

I gave people the benefit of the doubt. I accepted blind dates. I ignored my rule about not dating guys shorter than me. The point is, it's not like I wasn't trying.

I was sitting outside my favorite ice cream shop with my best friend (because sometimes you need ice cream—not wine), when I heard myself declare: "I'm never going to fall in love again." We'd been talking about watching my ex-boyfriend move on after our breakup. Hearing myself in that moment, it was as if my soul had separated from my body, proceeding to hover above my cake-batter cone as I uttered the most important piece of information available in the quest for my soul-mate.

There it was, right in front of me. Or shall I say: right inside of me. The piece of the puzzle I had been searching for. Why did I continue to hit wall after wall when it came to dating? Why wasn't anything sticking? Why did all the hot guys have drug problems—I mean, I lived in Miami, but still—why was I so unsuccessful in my search?

The answer? I never believed it was actually going to happen for me, and this was the kind of trust I'd find only inside myself.

THE ANSWERS ARE WITHIN US

You see, about a year prior, I went through a breakup. I was young, naive, and totally in love with this person, so I thought our relationship would last forever. Then he started to have a conversation with me one day that included the line, "It's not you, it's me" sandwiched somewhere in the middle, and I was in literal disbelief.

At some point in the relationship, I had convinced myself I was going to marry this person. My mind was made up. When it all came crashing down, it was very hard for my mind to recalibrate.

This is why breakups are so hard. Our mind has envisioned a future with this person. When that plan doesn't work out, the mind can't seem to imagine another future. It's a real trauma. This is also the reason we try to make it work with our ex-lovers, going back and forth for months and even years sometimes. Because there is no Plan B.

My mind was trying to come up with a new vision after I was dumped. Since my energy and self-esteem were at an all-time low, all I could come up with at the time was, "I'm never going to fall in love again." Like attracts like, so my low energy could only attract low-vibrational thoughts like this one. It was the next best future vision I could let my mind hold onto, ever since marrying my now-ex-boyfriend had ceased to be an option.

As a student of hypnotherapy and all things brain, I knew that our thoughts were powerful. So when I heard myself speak that day at the ice cream shop with my friend, angel voices sang. I was searching for an answer to why my dating life was such a circus. I looked at my strategy, thinking maybe I should get online more or ask for people to set me up. I changed my hair and tried to become thinner. I even became flexible with what I wanted from a partner. I was looking for answers outside of myself. Until finally, that day, I realized that the answer was not outside, but within me all along.

✳ The words I was using were the clues I was searching for. It showed me what I really believed my fate would be. Despite all the steps I was taking to find love, I was never going to find it because subconsciously what I really wanted was to never fall in love again.

I don't need to be psychic to know that you probably have some gnarly thoughts of your own, which is why you feel frustrated, disappointed, and maybe even hopeless. It's also the reason you're not meeting any winners, or maybe nobody at all.

✳ But you know what? There's great news here. It's working! The universe is listening and giving you what you believe. Now we need to get you believing in what *you* want. Have no fear. You got this.

IT **WILL** HAPPEN FOR YOU

Before we get into the technicality of changing our beliefs, allow me to remind you of something. Our desires are placed in our hearts because the outcome is part of our purpose. As we learn to work with our beliefs, so many of us feel guilty about wanting what we want. I'm here to tell you that what we want is of divine importance.

Your desire for a loving partnership is the call of your soul. When we have these kinds of wants, we can move forward with confidence knowing that the universe, our guides, our past loved ones, and all the loving energy of the world are on our side, doing what they can to help us fulfill a part of our purpose.

There's nothing pathetic about wanting a partnership. You are not a bad feminist for coupling up. In fact, you are very brave for wanting to share your life with someone, because relationships require a lot of spiritual work on our part. When we live life with someone else, we are asked time and time again to look at ourselves and evolve. Choosing to be alone, for those of us who are meant to seek partnership, can very well be the cowardly way out.

Whatever it is we desire, the universe will happily place it on a silver platter for us. No questions asked, no judgments. The universe isn't like Santa Claus, making a naughty and nice list and checking it twice. It's not looking at your desires and wondering if they're good or bad. It's not thinking that you should be punished because you had one too many one-night stands or were a bad wife to a good man at some point in the past.

The universe truly wants to give you what you desire. The reason I say this is because I want you to know that if you want a loving partnership, you will have it. In the deepest place of my soul, I know this to be true. Especially if you follow the steps in this book.

How do I know this? For starters, you're reading this book, which means you're an awesome, beautiful person who cares enough to look within themselves. That says a lot about you.

But even if you were someone who hated miniature giraffes, you would still find love. And the reason is that we live in a universe with pretty clear laws. For instance, what we think about obsessively becomes belief; it ultimately determines the form of *our lives.*

The way to feel as if we're living a meaningful life is by answering our souls' whispers. Since your soul is whispering for a beautiful, loving, romantic partnership, allow me to help you show up for the call. It begins with understanding your deepest beliefs.

DIGGING THROUGH THE MUD

The first step is learning about your own beliefs. Typically, when faced with this question, we don't know the answer. That's because there are subconscious beliefs and conscious ones—the kind that are hidden, and the kind on the surface.

A conscious belief might be that drinking water is good, or perhaps you believe that the word "ghosting" should be retired. These are things you know about yourself. These beliefs are out in the open and easily available for you to see, understand, and communicate.

Subconscious beliefs are the tricky ones, because sometimes we're not aware of them. This is the part of the mind that stores our past memories—the good, the bad, even the traumatic. These beliefs govern our behavior and ultimately create our personalities.

For our purposes, we're looking for the ones blocking you, but that doesn't mean all subconscious beliefs are negative. Our son's teacher believes he is the most artistic in the class, and she loves to remind him of this. One day, our four-year-old was coloring with pride as he said to me, "Mommy, I am an artist."

Is his coloring of the Incredible Hulk any more magnificent than any other child his age? We're not sure. But because his teacher has complimented him enough, he believes that he is an artist. As long as he has this belief, he will apply himself more in the arts and feel confident in that space. Ultimately, this belief will become part of his identity.

Then there are the not-so-great beliefs, like when we believe we're not young enough because our ex cheated on us with a younger woman. Or the belief that we're overweight because we carried some baby fat in the fifth grade and got teased about it on the playground. These are the beliefs we must find, but we also need to recognize those that once were great but perhaps no longer serve us.

Growing up, I was told that I could only make a living as a doctor, lawyer, or engineer. I was out to prove people wrong; I decided I would succeed no matter what. I was driven by the fear of failing—the fear of me being wrong and them being right. So I worked my butt off, climbing the ladder as a fashion and beauty writer, ultimately becoming an editor at several prestigious publications. I had a great resume and very little shame when it came to getting what I wanted in life.

But eventually I became exhausted, and I didn't want to do it anymore. Plus, my life seemed like a lot of accomplishments that didn't make me happy. All of my choices were based on how other people perceived me, rather than what actually filled my soul.

This is an example of when a belief spoils. "I will succeed no matter what," was a great belief for me for a while, but it grew in poor soil and ultimately became a weed blocking the potential for a happy life.

You may be wondering, why not skip the digging part and just pile on some new, positive beliefs? A lot of teachers and websites may recommend this strategy. This would be like planting a beautiful flower garden among a bunch of weeds. It won't be pretty.

If we don't do the work of digging through the junky beliefs, we have no idea what we're up against. When we don't know what is within us, we don't know who we are. And that's scary stuff. It's like having this monster living inside of us, but having no idea it's there. Like our pal Riri suggests, let's become *friends with the monster under our bed*, shall we?

4 EXERCISES TO HELP YOU UNCOVER YOUR BELIEFS

1. Journal

Every day for the next ten days, spend five uninterrupted minutes journaling your thoughts about dating. Don't judge the writing. Don't overthink it. Just let it flow from your heart. Once you're done, you can start observing what you wrote and asking yourself what it means to you.

You'll be surprised to find that so many of our unconscious beliefs aren't as hidden as we imagine. Below are some questions to help prompt you and get the words flowing. Before answering the questions, I want you to put your hand on your heart, close your eyes, take a deep breath, and set the intention for all your limiting beliefs to find themselves on the pages of your journal.

Will I be alone forever?
Will I ever find happiness?
Is there a person in my city who I can connect with?
Why haven't I found the partnership I've been looking for?
Who do I need to become to find this partnership?
Do I believe I'm good enough to be loved?
Is my heart ready for love?
What are my feelings about dating?
Are there any good people left out there?

2. Watch Your Language

Like the story about the ice cream shop, we literally speak our beliefs all day long. It's time to watch our language when we speak to girlfriends, moms, co-workers, and to whomever else we divulge our deepest secrets.

Honestly, it doesn't even need to be someone close. I remember going on a first date once (before meeting the ex-boyfriend) and telling the guy that I wanted to fall in love and feel crazy over someone. Guess who I met next? The ex-boyfriend who made me feel crazy. Be careful what you wish for, right?

The point is, if you practice a little bit of self-awareness, you'll find what is inside of you. If you say things like, "I'll never find a guy I like in this city," you might as well pack your bags and move. I am completely serious about this. If you believe there are no good guys in your city, your mind is going to be focused on finding examples to prove that theory right. What we believe is what we see.

No matter where you live, there's always a possibility of finding someone. People fly into where you live, don't they? Don't even get me started if you live in a big city! I can prove this belief wrong over and over again, but it doesn't matter if the statement is factually correct or incorrect. All that matters is that you believe it.

If you don't want to leave your city, you must believe that there's always a possibility of finding someone. If you feel in your heart that leaving is the right move for you, then that's ok, too—just know that you're not choosing to move due to a lack of eligible bachelors in your town; you're choosing to move to fulfil a separate desire of leaving your current location.

For the next week, set a timer on your phone for every two hours. Let that alarm be a reminder to observe the nature of your words. If you don't like the timer idea, leave post-it's reading, *Watch what you say* around your home, in your car, on your phone, or even on your desk.

3. Work With A Pro

If you find yourself feeling confused about this process, hire some help. It's worth it. A good hypnotist, therapist, or coach can help you uncover beliefs without too much effort. In my practice, I'm able to see limiting beliefs in one session. It's up to the client to work on them, but discovering the belief is half the battle.

4. Take a Look at Some Commonly Held Limiting Beliefs

Below is a list of common limiting beliefs that I often find within my clients. Read them over and see if any resonate with you.

I'll never find love again.

There are no good people left.

I'll never find someone in my city.

I'm not skinny enough yet.

I'm too old to find love.

Opening my heart to love is not safe.

People are afraid of my success or my drive and therefore won't date me.

Guys just want to mess around; they're not interested in a committed relationship.

Step Two:
FORGIVE

I once had a client who found some really great dating advice in a book she was reading. The book said that when we're ready for someone to come into our lives, we must make space for them. The author suggests we make space by sleeping on one side of the bed, adding an extra pillow as if already sharing our beds, or making one of our drawers off limits, as if someone already occupies it.

I can appreciate the exercise. I, too, believe we must create space before introducing something new; however, if you try to make space in your bed, probably all you'll learn from the exercise is that you need a bigger bed!

We do need to make space. But we need to make space within ourselves first. After years of dating and disappointments and just life in general, we've picked up baggage that no longer serves us. The baggage is weighing us down on the journey to love.

As we begin to do the dirty work of digging through our beliefs, we inevitably start to question the origins of our stickiest limiting thoughts. What we find is that some beliefs were given to us by a parent, teacher, bully, or even a friend. A mom who is angry about her husband leaving may raise her daughters to believe that men are not to be trusted, that women must learn to live alone. Or it could be a more recent belief that has stuck, like the kind we picked up during our last breakup, the belief that it's not safe to love. For this reason, we live life with a closed heart.

Discovering the births of our beliefs can release waves of anger and victim-based thinking. I do not want to discount your experience; in the past, you may very well have been victimized. You may have been the victim of your father's anger, your mother's jealousy, a bully's insecurity, and so on and so forth, but because of those experiences, you picked up some beliefs about yourself and the world, which now dictate your life.

Feeling sorry for ourselves is our way of self-mothering; that voice inside our heads comes from the mother, and there are various inner mothers. Some of us have a sergeant mom, who never allows us to rest or fail, while others have the lax mom, who let's us drown in our indulgences whenever things get tough. Perhaps you have a combination of the two, but for those of us still learning to love ourselves, that voice inside is rarely healthy.

Since we don't know how to show ourselves compassion while still believing in our own power, we think feeling bad for ourselves is the answer. This is how we comfort the pain we feel, but in reality, feeling like a victim only perpetuates the suffering. Being lied to and deceived by my ex-boyfriend made me angry that I even had to go through the agonizing pain of dating again. I was embarrassed by the fact that I was single, essentially *unlovable*, when all my friends were either married or talking about it.

I also felt wronged by my mother. She was my excuse for pretty much anything that I fell short on—from money and relationships to self-esteem. I couldn't seem to pick myself up, so I blamed my mom for not being there instead. This way of mothering myself felt good for awhile. Until it didn't.

I ultimately discovered tons of anger and sadness in my heart, and while they stemmed from real, factual experiences that hurt me once upon a time, those experiences only lasted a few minutes. Since I was unwilling to forgive, I turned those past moments into monsters orchestrating my future.

With the belief system of *I am a victim*, I had a very small chance of seeing anything besides what I believed. I continued to be "victimized" by my mother's actions, and I was dating men who were never going to make our relationship a priority. When we believe something so deeply, we want more than anything to prove ourselves right. I don't want this information to overwhelm you; on the contrary, I want you to see the potential. We always have power in these situations—the power of choice. You get to decide what you want to believe.

IT'S YOUR CHOICE

I make choosing our beliefs sound easy, but the truth is, it doesn't always feel easy. Especially when our minds and hearts are filled with emotionally-charged beliefs. Many times, the most damaging thoughts we keep were introduced to us by loved ones. If we realize that the teachings and feelings they imparted were completely false and hurtful, we easily become angered.

The first big realization is uncovering the beliefs sabotaging our happiness. That's always eye-opening. The next realization is discovering who or what taught us the belief. Getting over the fact that someone introduced such a damaging belief to us is often harder than getting over the belief itself.

I want to hold space for you and let you feel that hurt, but I don't want you to stay there. The longer you stay in resentment, the longer it takes to attract the loving relationship you seek.

You could find *someone* from where you are; you don't *need* this book, but you might not find the quality of person you deserve. You'll find someone with only half of their heart available, just like yours. The other half will be filled with resentment, hurt, fear, and a mess of limiting beliefs.

The universe often delays us from meeting someone before we do this internal work, as a method of protecting us from ending up in the wrong relationship. When we have lessons to learn, the universe teaches them to us in the area of our lives that matters the most. The universe is dangling the metaphorical carrot in our faces—mean, I know, but all we have to do is show up for the work.

Can we ever be completely empty of our negative beliefs? I've yet to find someone who is, but we can definitely tidy up. Forgiving and releasing is like owning the best vacuum on the market.

IT'S JUST THE BEGINNING

I know we might be moving a little fast. After all, you may have just discovered these thoughts, linking them with a person towards whom you already had ill-feelings. We can't force ourselves to forgive, but what we can do is set the intention.

All I ask is that we get the ball rolling. If you don't feel ready yet, in your prayers or conversations with the universe you can say, *I would like to begin to feel ready to forgive this person who hurt me*. You can also declare your desires: *I want to create space in my heart for the love I deserve*.

Whispering your desires and intentions into the world shows that you are willing to heal. The universe will meet you with kindness and guide you through the process. Do not be afraid; remember, we do not forgive others to let them off the hook. We're choosing to let go of our pain, but this does not mean we approve of their behavior. We don't need to be friends with this person nor run off into the sunset holding hands.

Forgiving is a gift we give ourselves. Until we decide to open the door to forgiveness, we allow others to hurt us over and over again. Each day, we give that person permission to hurt us. When we finally decide to forgive—or start forgiving—this person no longer has control over us. Our chance at happiness is no longer in their hands.

You deserve to be in control of your happiness. You deserve to love again. You deserve to receive real, lasting, compassionate love—and you deserve all of that without the shadow of resentment hanging over you.

FORGIVE HER TOO

Now that we're on the subject of what you deserve, you also deserve forgiveness for your own shortcomings and perceived mistakes.

It's often easier to forgive others and keep ourselves in the time-out corner. I get it. We like to hold ourselves to a higher standard because we think we should know better, but at the time of the offense, did we *really* know better?

My client Janet married a real winner (when I say winner, I mean total loser). There were signs of infidelity before they said "I do." Throughout the marriage, there were traces of his double life, but Janet failed to see it. She saw what she wanted; quite frankly, this was a survival tactic. They had two children and she was doing her best to keep the family together—so she looked the other way.

One day, it all came crashing down. She could no longer ignore the lies invading their lives. As she found herself going through divorce, she began to see her husband's true colors, finally facing up to the monster he'd always been. Rather than direct all that anger and blame towards him, she turned the lens on herself. She could not shake the feeling that it was her fault for trusting him, and she shouldered the responsibility for her children having such an awful father.

Like Janet, we often blame ourselves when it's not logical. Janet's husband was verbally abusive, calling her overactive and incapable of controlling her emotions. Basically, she felt like the crazy one. I think we can all see a piece of ourselves in Janet. At some point, someone has tried to squash our intuition and feelings for the sake of controlling us. If we haven't been taught another way, we often obey and believe we are the ones with the problem.

Of course, we all need to take accountability for who we allow into our lives, but blaming ourselves and holding ourselves accountable are two very different approaches. One hurts us, and the other empowers us to become more.

May I remind you that the person who made those past mistakes—be it hurting others, reckless sleeping around, or something else altogether—is a past version of yourself. She was doing the best she could with the information and experiences she had at the time. Of course, our wiser selves love to look back and judge our former selves for not knowing better, but the truth is: *she didn't know any better.* The reason you can look back now is because you grew from an experience that may have looked like a mistake, but in fact was part of the plan.

In an ideal world, we would go through life without experiencing failures or hurt, but without the contrast of the shadow, we cannot understand light. We sometimes need to experience the bad to know who we really are, what we want, and who we must become. Give yourself the love you deserve. Forgive yourself today. Vow to put the past behind you and extend compassion to your former self. In fact, thank her for the knowledge she found; accept her for who she was, who she is becoming, and the life she wants someday.

THE EX FACTOR

Speaking of crummy exes, let's talk about yours. Breakups are one of the hardest experiences I feel we can go through. I truly believe it's a real trauma for the mind. Think about it. When we date someone who we love long enough, our mind can't help but get attached. We start to envision a future with this person. We begin to make future plans with them in mind. Every time we look a few years down the road, we see this person there, until suddenly— poof—it's all gone.

Our hearts are broken, but our minds are also totally confused.

During your relationship, your mind began to believe that this was someone important, that all future visions should include him. When we experience a breakup, the brain is told, *scratch that*. Naturally, the mind needs time to come up with something new.

Breakups are hard. Loving someone who ultimately doesn't become your life partner is hard. Having to love someone new while dealing with an injured heart is hard, but you know what? It's possible.

You deserve to love again. In order to give yourself that opportunity, you have to put the ex behind you. You have to close that door. You may continue to care for them and think of them, but you're on the hunt for a true, loving partner. Your ex has proven not to be that.

In this process, you need to be selfish. It's an imperative process you're going through, and it matters. You deserve to go through it with a whole heart.

If you're still waiting for your ex to come back, I can almost guarantee you that the only path to reuniting is to truly close the door on the thought of being with him. You have to sincerely detach yourself, meaning, you have to believe there is no chance.

That break in your energy will serve you in two ways. Number one, you will be free to go through this process of dating without a heavy weight dragging you down. You'll date authentically, rather than as the hurt woman. Secondly, the ex will sense your distance, and if he was just trying to buy time before he committed to you, his fear of true distance from you will move him into action.

If he doesn't move into action, I truly believe there is someone better for you. I was so caught up on my ex-boyfriend; in my heart, he was *it*. A few years down the road, he made it very clear that he could not be what I wanted, yet I kept trying to see if he would change his mind.

Every day, I thank all the stars in the universe that my ex had the foresight to understand that what I wanted from a committed relationship would not work for him. After spending a few years in marriage and seeing how challenging it could be—especially when you throw kids into the picture—I now realize that the universe was protecting me when my former relationship fell apart.

You, my friend, were being protected. The past fell apart to give you a second chance. Now that you're reading this book, you can draw someone in from a pure place. It is the greatest gift you can give yourself.

I know you might resist my perspective. You may want to tell me that you and your ex are soulmates or meant to be, but that belief is pretty basic. My clients often ask me if they're "meant to be" with someone in particular. They constantly wonder if fate has anything to do with their chance at love, or if soulmates are even a real thing.

The reason we feel particularly attached to a person is often because we're soulmates. You've done this before with them. There is a level of familiarity that feels comfortable, but that doesn't mean the relationship was meant to last for an entire lifetime. This is where we go wrong.

First of all, we encounter many soulmates in this lifetime. It doesn't mean we need to marry all of them! Soulmates are souls we've lived with in another lifetime. Your sister, father, best friend, or boss may all be soulmates.

Even your most challenging relationships may be with soulmates. Oftentimes we make agreements with these souls to learn lessons together.

Your ex may very well have been a soulmate who came into your life to work through a lesson together, to complete some karma, or even help with the expansion of your soul. In a way, these relationships give us a glimpse into the spirit world, and it feels really good, so we try to hold on for as long as possible.

When we feel this cosmic connection, we think the relationship is supposed to last forever. In reality though, once the karma is completed, the relationship will disintegrate on purpose, because you're ready to move on in your soul's evolution.

Know that the past relationship played out exactly as intended. The misunderstanding occurred when we started to believe it was supposed to last longer. That's just us trying to control our fate, and as we know, when we insist on control, we end up losing.

Oftentimes, we try to hold onto our past loves, believing that they're our one shot at happiness or true love. Right there, you can see there's a flaw in our thinking. One person is in charge of our complete happiness, meaning that happiness is outside of us?

Instead, you want to believe that no matter who ends up being your partner, you'll find a true, loving relationship. Your goal is to find true love, not get back with your ex. If you set your focus on your ex, you may get him back, but that doesn't mean you've found true love.

For this reason, I always recommend taking a higher perspective. You need to be very clear on what you want. When you get down to it, you'll see that what you want is not your ex-boyfriend, but rather a feeling. That feeling can be security or the feeling of being desired and so on.

My client Kristina was having an affair. Before you judge her, she was deeply unhappy in her marriage and didn't have the emotional intelligence to sort things out. She was feeling a lot of lack, so she tried to find it outside of herself and her own marriage.

Her new guy made her feel loved, appreciated, and like a free spirit. Naturally, she was trying to understand if it was meant to be with her new fling, or if she should work things out with her husband. I explained to Kristina that she didn't fall in love with the new guy, but the woman she became when she was around him. He gave her the space to be who she was—full of emotions, sensual, and adventurous.

I mention this story because we often think we fall in love with the guy, but really, we fall in love with a version of ourselves we have yet to meet. Ask yourself whether the reason you miss your ex is because you miss the person you were with him, because *that* person you can definitely get back, and you won't even need to compromise.

4 EXERCISES FOR RELEASING THE PAST

When we're looking to forgive, oftentimes we don't know where to start. Since we forgive people in order to set ourselves free, and not to help them, there's no need to call them up and announce, "By the way, I forgive you." Frankly, they most likely don't care, but we do feel the need to do something. To purge. To release. To breathe.

I believe in performing a tangible task to help us with releasing the intangible. Next are five exercises you can perform to assist you in letting go of all you're ready to release.

1. Cleaning House

Out with the old and in with the new! That's exactly what we accomplish when we forgive and purge old beliefs. All this internal work changes our energy, making it clear, light, and of a higher vibration. That's exactly the kind of energy we want when dating, because it gives us the best possibility for meeting someone.

One simple activity that really makes a difference is cleaning out your space. Whether you live in a house, an apartment, or simply a room, you will see a big change in perspective by getting rid of the items in your home that hold stagnant energy. I'm talking to you—yes, *you* with the old t-shirt from your high school boyfriend.

Look around your space. Any piece that does not make you feel energized, give it away. Anything that doesn't represent who you are or want to become, let it go.

And if you want extra credit, leave space where you can. Leave an empty shelf in the kitchen or an empty drawer somewhere. We do this to remind ourselves that we don't have to crowd our lives to feel secure. It's important to get used to having space. It's vital that we get comfortable with silence. That way, we leave space for something new to come into our lives, something that makes us happier.

Block out a day this week to clean your house and feel yourself get lighter and more energetic.

2. Releasing with Fire

For this exercise, you'll need a safe way to burn a piece of paper. Grab yourself a cooking pot if need be! You'll also need paper, pen, and some kind of flame.

This ritual is best done on a full moon to take advantage of the moon's natural powers during this phase. But any time is good to forgive and release the past.

Grab your paper and think of the person you want to forgive. On that piece of paper, write down exactly how that person or situation made you feel. Leave all your hurt feelings on the page. Don't hold back. Let your body expose the toxic feelings with language. If you need a few papers, that's okay!

Once you have written the whole story, I want you to crumble the paper(s). Then, while it's still in your hand, repeat the following phrase:

"I release and forgive you.
And by doing this, I set myself free.
I am free."

Toss the paper into the fire and imagine all the negativity leaving your body and smoldering into ashes.

3. Energy Cords

This is going to sound creepy, but did you know that people can attach energy cords to us? Imagine an energetic umbilical cord coming from you and attaching to your ex. I know. Gross, right?

When we have these intense relationships with people (not just romantic), sometimes we create energetic attachments, making it hard to move on when necessary. I see them all the time in my sessions in all sorts of places, but have no fear, you can clear them out no problem.

What you want to do is sit in meditation, close your eyes, and ask that Archangel Michael come work with you. Archangel Michael is known for his skills in releasing negative energy and protecting us from the darkness. He is the archangel best known for his fear-zapping powers.

Ask him to cut any cords you may have. Repeat the phrase, *I am ready to release these energetic cords to the light.* Take a deep breath, and imagine him cutting cords attached to your energetic body.

Warning: the ex may reach out, because the people who leave cords on us actually miss them once they're cut.

4. Bathe

Since most of us bathe every day, we tend to forget how water cleanses our physical and energetic bodies. When we're intentional with our baths, we clear out much of the negative energy and thoughts we carry. Plus, it's a simple practice that we can do almost anytime.

New York-based shaman, Deborah Hanekamp, also known as Mama Medicine, does beautiful work with bath rituals and often shares her recipes on Instagram (@mamamedicine). During the Equinox, she posted one "potion" that she created to help bring ourselves back to balance. She generously agreed to allow me to include the recipe in this book.

What you'll need is:

+ Blue Majik
+ Rose quartz crystal
+ Rose Absolute essential oil
+ Epsom salt
+ Red roses

Steps to perform the ritual:
Cleanse your aura with the smoke of white sage.
Step into the bath and dunk your head underwater.
Release by doing several rounds of ujjayi breathing, with an equal balance of inhaling and exhaling. Inhale your love and

exhale your love.

Sit and soak in the medicine you created.

5. Shake it Off

I love all the practices I mentioned above, but the one that's most crucial is movement. We can spend years in talk therapy and truly believe we've overcome our baggage. Then one day, we find ourselves in yoga class opening our hips and simultaneously bursting into tears.

The body holds all our hurts—not just the physical ones, but the emotional ones, too. If we do not release them through our bodies, they manifest themselves in physical form. We must move the energy through our bodies in order to expunge the old from ourselves.

Find yourself a good tribal beat with drums, something that makes you want to move your body in the most primitive way. Make noises if you want. Allow your body to release and create that space you've been craving.

Step Three:
GET CLEAR

I'll be honest with you...when I was deep into my dating marathon, most of my friends thought I was a wild child with a dash of slut. Showing up with a different guy to every social gathering gives you that reputation.

On the surface, I was all over the place, but really this was my strategy. You see, I learn by contrast. Growing up, my mom used to protect me from messing up, but I begged her not to control me because I learned from my mistakes. While this never went over well with my mom, the same philosophy has rung true for me over many years.

When I was dating, I would test out a bunch of guys to see who I liked and who I didn't, but I learned this strategy the hard way. Remember that story I told you about how I almost married my high school sweetheart?

I'm thankful I didn't, because I'm almost positive that I would now be writing about my experience with divorce. When I was with him, I was constantly curious about other men. It was like I was brought to an amazing bakery where I could only have the blue cupcake on the top shelf. Everything else was off limits. I don't know about you, but I'm the kind of girl who needs to try all the sweets before committing to just one. Testing, trying, and failing is how we narrow down what we want in a partner.

After I broke up with my high school sweetheart, my instinct was to jump right into another relationship. The feeling of being without a boyfriend was foreign to me after coming out of an eight-year-long relationship. When feelings are foreign, our default is to make the feeling go away rather than sit back until it dissolves.

I tried really hard to force relationships, but thankfully none of them worked. I was clueless as to what I really wanted in a relationship. Of course, at the time I was frustrated and confused about why nothing worked for me, but looking back I understand this was where I needed to be. It's moments like these that remind us that sometimes there's a greater plan for us than that which we try to enforce.

As much as we want a perfect formula to follow to avoid being hurt, we also learn a lot from trial and error. All those gnarly beliefs and hurtful experiences serve a purpose; they create sets of priorities in our desires.

After we create space by acknowledging and releasing the beliefs that no longer serve us, the next step is getting clear on what we want. It's not enough to replace the old thoughts with generic positive thoughts. We want to introduce new thoughts to our brains, ones that will help us get where we want.

We also want to become clear on our intentions, because knowing what we want makes the whole dating process much more fun. Sometimes we wander around, allowing the universe to give us whatever it wants, and we call this "going with the flow." However, we forget that the universe is on our side; it wants to give us what we need. We ask through our beliefs. If we believe all men are cheaters, the universe will provide us with the requisite proof.

For this reason, we want to align our beliefs with our desires for partnership. We want to create beliefs that reflect what we want in our lives. If we want to see a loving, loyal relationship, we must download beliefs that produce that kind of possibility, saving them to the hard-drive of our minds.

You may be thinking, "Well, isn't that trying to control or play God?" In fact, this is you listening to God, because desires are nestled in the soul by the Spirit. The things we want, especially those we work so hard for—those things we can't let go of—are part of our soul's plan. We have to finish the work by learning how to play the games of the universe and fulfilling our initial desires. The system is designed for us to learn to heal and step into our power to create.

I do believe our pure desires come from an intuitive understanding of our soul's contract. When we continue to pursue something, despite the pain it causes, it's because part of us knows this journey belongs to the work we were called to do in this lifetime. Your pursuit to find love is part of your purpose.

Can this tool of implanting beliefs come with poor intentions? Of course, but the same theory applies to using a knife to stab someone instead of cooking a nurturing meal. The darkness uses the same tools we use to create both good and bad in the world. Your desire to bring love into your life is not bad. You are not trying to manipulate anyone if you're reading this book. So you can trust that your desire is pure and part of a greater purpose.

When we're part of a loving relationship, we have the potential to create beauty. When two people come together in the name of love, it's good for the entire world. A union of love is the seed that creates more love in the world. Romantic relationships are an opportunity to heal and love ourselves more deeply. When we empty and love ourselves, we show up as better humans, which ultimately makes this world a better place.

So please, never doubt your desires. Don't underestimate your calling to find real, lasting love. Take the time to read this book, heal yourself, and call up what your soul needs; you'll be making the world a better place. You have the capacity to create so much beauty, but it begins with a clear understanding of what you want from a partnership.

POWER OF INTENTIONS

We can have two separate intentions and still desire the same thing. For example, your intention behind wanting a relationship may be because you want to share your already beautiful life with someone, or because you feel having someone by your side makes you complete. Neither intention is better than the other, nor is either bad. Both intentions will produce a relationship. But the relationships will be very different.

I see intentions as the energy we send into the world. Close your eyes and imagine that your intentions have certain vibrations. These vibrations enter the world looking for other vibrations just like themselves. Once these like vibrations find each other, they make connections; suddenly the vibration lasts longer.

The intention of *I want a romantic relationship because I want to share my beautiful life with someone,* has its own vibration. Once that intention is let loose on the world, it seeks out a similar vibration, in the form of a person, who loves their life and wants to share it with another happy person, too.

The intention of *I want a romantic relationship because I want to feel complete,* has another vibration. It, too, seeks its respective match, searching for vibrations from people who also feel incomplete. We often don't understand intentions, and therefore we don't understand why we attract the wrong people, such as those who need to be fixed. If we go back a few months, before we met the person who needed fixing, often we see that our intention with dating was to find someone who needed us. After all, someone who needs us will not leave us.

We rarely do this deep work before dating. For this reason, five years after meeting the person of our dreams, we find ourselves married to someone who cannot get it together. If we do this work early on, setting our intentions with clarity, we avoid a lot of unnecessary suffering later.

WHAT DO YOU WANT?

Here's a question for you: what do you really want? Maybe you know exactly what you want. Maybe you know exactly what you don't want, or maybe you're just beginning to figure it out.

In my experiences with failed relationships, I dated this one guy who wouldn't let me in. I'm a really good helper, which he absolutely needed, but it was completely frustrating to experience him resisting my help. I felt like our lives were being lived and planned independently.

From that relationship, I learned that I wanted to be with someone who I could help and would help me, like real partners do. Fast-forward to present day, and my husband is always looking for my involvement in his entrepreneurial ventures. Be careful what you wish for! All joking aside, feeling like partners was important to me, so I set that intention.

We all want and need different things. Feeling secure might be big for you, but the next girl might need a lot of change and excitement. It really doesn't matter what you want; what matters is identifying it. The more you know and honor yourself—meaning you don't judge yourself for being a certain way—the better you become at identifying your needs in a relationship. Never be too cool to admit what you want.

My client Jessica dated this guy for eight years. When they met, she wasn't looking for anything serious. She was in a stage of her life where she enjoyed her independence and had a good time with friends.

One night, while she was out dancing at Miami's hottest club, she and her future boyfriend caught eyes. He, too, was enjoying life, but as they got to know each other, they decided they wanted to have more fun together, instead of apart.

Jessica was the only girl in a family of five. Growing up with brothers who told stories about "needy" and "demanding" girls, Jessica vowed to never be that way. Instead, she gave off a vibe that everything was "cool" with her, which was exactly what her fun-loving boyfriend wanted when they met.

The years continued to go by; Jessica and her boyfriend stayed together, but he was obviously not the right fit. Although Jessica liked to have fun, she also loved being present with her loved ones, attending family and friend functions often. Her boyfriend did not value those relationships as much as she did. Jessica also wanted to marry and have kids one day. Her boyfriend did not show any signs of wanting the same things, but because Jessica feared appearing as nagging or "uncool," she never spoke up about what she wanted in a relationship.

As their eight-year anniversary neared closer, Jessica realized that her friends were all married or pregnant. She knew this would go on forever, unless she confronted what she honestly wanted from a romantic relationship.

Typically, we look at a relationship like this and judge the boyfriend. *Why isn't he proposing? Why won't he show up to family functions?* When the truth is, coupling up means selling ourselves in a particular way. We make energetic commitments that stem from our intentions, and these form far before we meet our partners.

Jessica made an energetic commitment to her boyfriend that she would remain easy-going and self-sufficient. Energetically, her boyfriend accepted. In fact, it was exactly what he was looking for; he didn't know any better. Until Jessica was ready to be honest about her desires, her boyfriend was left in the dark, continuing to act as if nothing was wrong in their relationship.

Being honest about what we need in a relationship, and later setting clear intentions, saves us from a lot of misunderstanding. I truly believe that you have yet to find the right person for you, because if you were to have found someone without being aware of your intentions and desires, the relationship would be a total mess. You, my friend, have dodged a bullet. Going forward, you're going to get it right.

THE LIST

Guess what I'm going to make you do next? It's time to create a "perfect man" checklist. Before you close this book and demand your money back, hear me out. This list is going to serve several purposes.

First, it will allow you to see what you really want. Second, you'll learn *why* you want it, which helps when you're ready to set intentions. Lastly, the list will serve as a commitment to yourself. It's so easy to get exhausted by the dating process. Instead of settling for the first person that comes along, this list prevents us from going too far with people who don't fit our needs.

Grab your notebook, open to a blank page, and start writing out the qualities you want in a partner. Don't be shy. If you want tall, dark, handsome, and rich, write it out. Ain't no shame in this game. Be as specific as possible.

THE WISDOM OF WANTING

You might be thinking, "I've made this list before, only to realize that I have very high standards." It's never worked in the past, right? Well, that's because your strategy needs some tweaking.

Typically, our list is full of outside things. We're looking at the exterior. *I want him to be tall, wealthy, kind, family-oriented, and so on.*

Again, there's nothing wrong with wanting these things, but one desire can be driven by different intentions. The desire will manifest itself, but the intention is what dictates its shape. For that reason, the secret to making a successful list is including the intention behind each attribute you desire.

The idea for creating a list came from my own dating experience.

Like most women in the dating scene, I received the advice to create a list of what I wanted—which, by the way, felt oddly similar to the concept of writing to Santa. After coming home from yet another unsuccessful night of bar hopping with my friends, I decided to throw up the little white flag and take out my journal. I jotted down everything I wanted in a potential partner and included phrases like:

taller than me with heels
has a good job that makes good money
good-looking
lets me help
drives a nice car
lives in a nice place
is looking to commit
creative

I closed my journal, tucked it away, and didn't think much of what I wrote. A few months later, I met my husband. After a few dates, I knew the relationship was going to be serious, and I couldn't handle it; instead I tried to find flaws in my partner and our relationship.

At the time, I was learning about the law of attraction, trying hard to control my thoughts and call in the right relationship. In fact, the list was supposed to be part of this process. When my husband showed up in my life, I thought, *I must be doing this attraction stuff all wrong.* The package he showed up in was hardly what I expected for my perfect mate. I thought the universe was going to bring me a boyfriend packaged in a perfect red bow. In other words, I was looking for exterior signs to prove that he was, in fact, the right fit for me.

Back then, my husband drove a pickup truck, lived in the suburbs, ran a business that sounded foreign to me, cared for his daughter, and seemed neither creative nor trendy. I was very snobby about this stuff. At the time, I was a fashion editor living in the heart of the city. I was used to dating tortured artists who drove hipster cars and lived with their parents—but they dreamt of living somewhere cool one day, and this was enough for me. So when my husband showed up acting all adult, I thought, *What is going on with my attracting skills?*

After a few dates with my husband, I was terrified. I could feel where this relationship was going, yet my ego couldn't handle how it appeared on the outside. I began to flake the next few times he asked me out, and ultimately he understood the signs. After that experience, I had a conversation with the universe in my mind.

"Dude, was I not clear with my list?
I said creative, nice car, nice place, good job that makes money."

A few weeks later, the universe responded. I met this really good-looking guy who lived in a beautiful high-rise building and drove a fancy car. I agreed to go on a date with him, and to my surprise, he was a very nice, loving guy.

As the dates continued, I quickly started to feel the red flags. He was the epitome of someone who dresses themselves up on the outside to hide how they feel on the inside. Family problems, recovering drug addict, bad with money, you name it. I didn't intend to judge, but he had so much to heal; I couldn't walk on that journey with him. Thankfully, I realized this and made my exit after just a few dates.

Frustrated with God, the universe, and the guides who supposedly were walking this path with me, I sat in my room wondering where I'd gone wrong. I truly felt ready for a relationship, yet I kept meeting all these ill-fitted men. Out of nowhere, I heard this voice inside of me say *look at the list*. I grabbed my journal and found the list, feeling immediately discouraged because the list did not represent the nature of my life.

Or did it? My list was about exterior traits: height, house, car, etc. Yet, my intentions behind my desires were not clear to me nor the universe. I was out there dating and sending multiple vibrations into the world, which meant attracting multiple types of people and scenarios.

As a student of the laws of attraction, I had to get clear on the intentions behind my desires. That's when I decided to revise the list by making it more feminine. My former list was very masculine, rigid; it came from my mind. In the revised list, I consulted with my heart and added in why I wanted what I wanted.

As it turns out, my heart's intentions were already speaking out to the universe. In fact, those intentions attracted my husband—you know, that guy with the pickup truck, zero edge, and plenty of adult-like charm—but because I was focused on all these exterior aspects of a person, I completely missed the point.

When I focused on outside appearances, I did not notice that he had everything on my initial list. He did have a nice car. He did live in a nice place. He was creative. The problem was that I had an idea of how those things were supposed to look. I thought a nice place was a high-rise apartment (most of which were probably leased and not owned by these guys) and a nice car was a convertible. Did you know that a nice pickup truck can be just as expensive as a top-of-the-line luxury sedan? That was news to this city girl.

After making list number two, I realized what my true intentions were, and from that I understood that the guy with the truck (my now-husband) was what I was looking for all along. And yes, I had to ask him for a second chance a few months after dismissing him for being too adult. Let's just say there was some stalking involved that I am not proud of.

When we focus on the exterior, we close a lot of doors that could have been potential matches. We cannot spot the right people when we're looking for exterior signs, and for that reason our options are limited.

LEADING WITH HEART

Faced with internal struggle, we often hear the advice, *Go with your heart*—which sounds beautiful and should come with a side of sprinkle-covered rainbows—but the truth is we rarely know what our hearts want. That's why we're struggling in the first place!

We often spend so much time in our heads, rather than our hearts; even when it comes to dating, which funny enough is a matter of the heart. Ideally we should lead with the heart, but since we rarely know where to start, the list becomes our greatest tool.

Intentions are the language of our hearts. They're the vibration of whatever we feel. Since we know intentions bring our desires to life, we need to understand our feelings around what we desire. We need to understand the wisdom of our wants.

We can start this process by looking at *what* we want. That's what the list is for, so look at everything you have written down. One by one, ask yourself why you want those certain traits. Notice that behind every trait you want, there's a feeling you want to fulfill.

The reason you want someone good-looking is not because you

are vain; it's because you want to *feel* attracted to them. You want to *feel* excited about getting physical with someone. The reason you might have "someone with stable finances" on your list is for want of security and equal partnership, not because you're a gold-digger.

To give you a head start with this assignment, below is a list of common traits I see on these lists. I've listed the trait and the possible feeling behind the trait, helping you to clarify your intentions.

Desire	Intention
I want someone who:	I want to feel:
is tall	*feminine and small in his arms*
is attractive	*attracted to someone*
likes to travel	*free to be adventurous and curious*
has a good family	*belonging and acceptance*
is honest	*safe trusting them*
is loyal	*like we're partners*

Here are some other common feelings we search for in partners, which the traditional list cannot quite express:

I want to feel like a priority
I want to feel understood
I want to feel desired
I want to feel attractive
I want to feel taken care of

INTENTIONS GONE WRONG

Not only is this process helpful in bringing us what we want, it also keeps us safe. When creating our lists of desires and intentions, sometimes we realize that our intentions are slightly off, causing us to attract the wrong person.

Lucy made her list one day with her girlfriends. She was that little girl who loved making Christmas lists, so when it came to asking the universe for what she wanted, she was totally game for the assignment. In her list, she was very specific, asking for a man with a boat who wore a suit and had, among other things, a vacation home. The universe responded by granting her a boyfriend with those exact qualifications.

Lucy found out two years later that none of these things belonged to him, even the job he wore a suit to wasn't real. It was all for show. When they eventually broke up, Lucy had to confront how the relationship turned out this way. What could she do to avoid something like this in the future? What came to mind was her original list.

Lucy and I talked about how the list goes wrong if we're not clear about intentions, admitting that she did want those things at the time—the boat, the vacation home, the suit—but only because she wanted to keep up appearances. Her intention and vibration indicated an importance in showing off, so she found someone else with the same rhythm. Someone who also felt that his value came from how his life appeared.

If she'd understood her intentions when making the list, she could have reworked things to attract both the boat and someone honest. She could have stopped herself and said, "No, I don't need these things because I want people to see me a certain way. I want them for me. I want them because I like the water and having a place to retreat to with someone I love." From that place, she would have attracted a great guy, plus the boat and the vacation home—and perhaps she could have let go of the suit.

The work of getting clear on intentions protects us. It can seem like hard work, but it's a worthy investment. For those of us who want the whole shebang—marriage, kids, house, etc—picking the right person is very serious business. Your relationship is the seed that ultimately sprouts in the other areas of your life. If you don't put any real thought into picking your seed, you may end up with a faulty tree somewhere down the line.

We often forget the importance of this process. Dating feels like a waiting game where we linger around until someone chooses us, but that is not the case. When you date, you don't wait for someone to pick you. You consciously go through a process of picking the right relationship for you. The other person chooses you, too, but both of you come to an agreement.

I know it doesn't always feel that way; I clearly remember sitting at a bar with my girlfriends, looking around like adulthood was a high school dance and I the proverbial *wallflower*. Once I understood that dating wasn't about waiting, but choosing, I was instantly empowered; the entire process became fun.

Creating the list with clear intentions is not only the first step to attracting the love of your life, but having fun with the often dreaded process of dating. Let's get started with that list, shall we?

3 STEPS TO CREATING YOUR LIST

For reference, here is the three-step process again:

1. List out everything you want from a romantic relationship. Don't be shy; aim for specificity.
2. For every desire, ask yourself, *Why?* Why do you want what you want?
3. Revise your initial list by creating another list, based on the feelings you want from a romantic relationship. Start each line with the phrase, "I want to feel…"

Step Four:
REPLACING THE BELIEF

Great news! You've made it past the hard part. Acknowledging our beliefs, releasing them, and getting clear on desires can be exhausting. You deserve a nap.

Know how amazing you are for making it through the first three chapters. Most people are not willing to do the deep work. Instead, their energy is full of junk; they fall in love with whomever eases their wounds. But you, my friend, you know better. I applaud and thank you on behalf of the world, because doing this work makes the planet a better place for everyone.

That said, don't rest on your laurels just yet. Now that we've shed as much light as possible on what you need from a romantic partnership, it's time to actually make it happen. The first step is replacing old beliefs with new ones that match your desires.

In order to attract the relationship you're hoping for, you have to believe that it's actually a possibility for you. You may want all those things you wrote on the list, but you may not believe you can have them, and that's where manifesting gets tricky. Have no fear, though, we're about to download some new, positive beliefs to get you where you want to be.

Introducing a generic positive belief does not work; instead, look at what you must believe to attract a particular desire. For example, let's say you want to attract a loving partnership but don't believe there are good men in your city. However, you also have no plans of moving away, so you're basically stuck.

In that scenario, what we want to do is change the belief: "There are no good men in my city." That said, if we simply replace the limiting belief with "I will find a loving relationship," we hit roadblocks because we haven't addressed the crux of our underlying beliefs. Instead, try to change the belief to something like, "This city is filled with so many different kinds of people, surely I'll meet someone who is perfect for me," or whatever feels right for you.

Again, we do this because our minds believe what they see. By downloading these new beliefs, you open new doors of opportunity that didn't exist before. There may even be an eligible partner working on the same floor as you, but because your mind believes there are no good men in your city, it finds men who validate this theory.

The same is true for the opposite. Now that your mind believes: "There are plenty of great men in this city, surely one of them is waiting for me," it finds you examples of compatible men in your area. This is not magic, but a change in perspective. You must work to see things differently in your life.

Let's play a little game. I want you to look around wherever you are for the color green, but only look for green.

Did you find a lot of green, or perhaps some green you'd never noticed? Depending on your focus, maybe you thought the room was mostly grey. Perhaps you were surprised to find a new color simply from focusing a different way.

This is exactly what we do with beliefs. It's not that you were wrong about the number of great guys in your city. There could be a lot of men who are not a good fit for you, which means you must work harder to notice the men who are. You fail to see the green because all you've been looking for is grey.

6 STEPS FOR CREATING NEW BELIEFS

Remember that soul seeking in step one, as we looked at our limiting beliefs? We need those now. Grab your journal and let's start replacing those beliefs with new ones.

1. Draw a line straight down the middle of your page, making two columns.
2. In the first column, make a list of the limiting beliefs you found in chapter one.
3. In the second column, write down the opposite belief of your limiting belief. Example, "I'll never fall in love again" vs. "I will fall in love again soon."
4. Once you're done with the limiting beliefs, go back to your desires, the list where you wrote down how you want to feel.
5. Write down how you want to feel in the left column, underneath the limiting beliefs.

6. To the right of your "how I want to feel" statements, write down what beliefs would protect that desire. Example, "I want to feel like a priority," or "I am worthy of being with someone who makes me a priority in their life."

Column One

I'll never fall in love again

I'm not skinny enough yet

I'm not sure this dating thing is working

I want to feel safe to trust

I want to feel like a priority

Column Two

I will fall in love again soon

I am worthy of love for who I am right now

I will find a loving partnership

It is safe to open up my heart to love

I deserve someone who puts me first

Step Five:
THE PURSUIT OF BELIEF

It's really sweet to write down these positive beliefs, isn't it? There's only one problem: you don't believe what you wrote—just yet, at least.

Believing is seeing. Believing is also a choice. Wouldn't it be great to trust that everything will work out? I know you want to believe, but you may not know how. First step? We must find the desire to change our minds.

When believing in something new, many of us experience resistance, for the same reason we hang onto old, frumpy sweaters. Although they don't fit anymore, in a weird way they make us feel safe. Believing something new means change. Change brings the unknown, and that can be very scary for those of us who try to control everything.

This process can be very uncomfortable, like waking up one day in someone else's clothes. We don't feel like ourselves, but let's be honest, was your old self serving your pursuit of love? Presumably not, if you're still reading this book.

Imagine you're a caterpillar busting from its cocoon and becoming what it always wanted: a butterfly. Or maybe the cocoon feels too safe and warm, so you devise a plan for staying there as long as possible.

Accepting the new beliefs that lead you to your soulmate is going to feel uncomfortable. You will want to retreat to your cocoon—the old habits. But you must remember that like any new habit, ultimately, the uncomfortable begins to feel comfortable.

You want to keep your eye on the prize. You're doing all this gritty work to be happy. Happiness comes from manifesting the desires etched in your soul, one of which is a romantic relationship, but you need a change of perspective to get there. That's why we're doing this work.

At this point, your mind may retreat to a place of *Why me? Why is it that other people don't have to read a book like this or attend some workshop in order to find love? Why do some people just happen to sit next to their future partner on an airplane?* I have an answer for you: it's all about the lesson.

Everyone has lessons to work through in this lifetime. Some of us work on jealousy, worth, humility, and so on. Whatever lesson you must learn through dating is one you've probably been trying to overcome in all areas of your life. This ain't your first rodeo.

Sometimes we avoid facing a certain lesson for a while, but ultimately it shows up in other meaningful areas of our lives. For example, the man who doesn't know his worth might avoid learning to love himself, which shows up in his finances. To make enough money, he must learn to know his worth, and since not making enough money is painful, he decides to embrace the work around his lesson and abolish the pain of being underpaid.

The pain of not having what you want needs to be stronger than the pain you anticipate coming from change. Are having to stop being the victim, love yourself, forgive, and so on, the most painful changes in your world? Or is life more painful without a loving partnership? You get to choose.

If living life without a fateful loving partnership is more painful than doing the work required to evolve, please read on. If you're too afraid of the unknown to move ahead, know that this lesson will show up in other areas of your life. You can run, my friend, but you cannot hide.

Let's just nip it in the bud and be open to change. You don't need to master the lesson in order to overcome it. The lesson may last a lifetime, but it begins now. I know I'm constantly working to remind myself that I'm enough. Releasing self-doubt is big for me; I have not mastered it and may not do so in this lifetime, but I've committed to work through the lessons, even if I fall on my face every time. This willingness to work is all we need to succeed.

Maybe you're afraid? Maybe somewhere inside, you doubt this will work? It doesn't matter. It's about the willingness, because taking steps to change and evolve even when we're terrified is the very definition of courage. It's also the definition of faith. When we take steps despite knowing the outcome, we plant small seeds of faith. They may not be fully grown, mature plants, but they're the beginning.

If you need to walk through this process with eyes closed and knees shaking, that's okay. I will hold your hand; know that faith lies in the willingness to act without knowing where you're heading. The steps will guide you into believing something new.

Some of your beliefs have been with you since childhood,

and introducing a new belief that challenges the old one can feel completely wrong. I ask that when your body tries to reject some of these new beliefs, talk yourself through it. Remind yourself that feeling uncomfortable is a good thing; you don't need to run and hide just yet. Instead, try sitting with that discomfort a moment; take several deep breaths and feel yourself come out of it anew.

HOW NEW BELIEFS STICK

At this point, you should have a list of new beliefs to replace the old ones, but that doesn't guarantee they're going to stick. The old beliefs actually found their place in your head after a lot of repetition and convincing. We absorb phrases, and if we repeat them enough in our minds, they become belief.

Sometimes we do this energetically but not verbally. For example, perhaps your mother never actually said you were less pretty than other girls, but she thought it enough that your feelings picked up her opinion. This was enough to make you intuitively know she didn't think you were the prettiest—not in the family nor the classroom.

After experiencing that feeling several times, you absorbed your mother's energy and made it your own. Now whenever life proves your theory correct, like your middle school crush going after your best friend, you repeat the phrase "I'm not pretty" to yourself. You do this so much that the thought becomes a toxic belief.

As an adult, dating is hard when you don't feel pretty. To offset this belief, you may have told yourself that you're the smart one, not the pretty one—you've lived your life identifying with the brain. You believe it's all you have to offer, so you lead with intellect, making sure the guy knows how smart you are. There's nothing wrong with smart, but the guy also wants to see your soft side. You only feel safe when it comes to matters of the mind. The heart feels vulnerable, so you don't allow yourself to go there. You and the guy never connect; you blame it on the fact that men are intimidated by smart girls, but that's not really the problem.

Evidently, beliefs take so many weird twists and turns; they cannot form overnight. They require convincing and repetition. In order to get these new beliefs to stick, we need the same kind of repetition every day—think of this as going to the gym for your brain.

3 STEPS FOR DOWNLOADING NEW BELIEFS

1. Repeat Your Mantras

You may already know what mantras are, but perhaps you don't know how to employ them. Mantras were created to give meditators focus in their practice, which has gone beyond Hinduism and Buddhism and entered the realm of changing thoughts. By repeating mantras over and over again, the phrase communicates with the unconscious mind, where our beliefs exist. With enough repetition, the mantra becomes our new belief, same as how the "negative" phrase becomes its own belief through repetition.

To find your mantras, head back to your latest list with the two columns. All the phrases in Column Two are possible mantras. Pick those that stick out to you and work on them one-by-one. Which beliefs created the biggest *aha* moment for you? You'll want to focus on those first.

You're going to repeat these phrases to yourself as much as you can. Remember in the book, *Green Eggs and Ham*, how Sam-I-Am gets Joey to eat his favorite dish in tons of weird places, until finally he likes them? Well, your mantras are your Green Eggs and Ham.

You can repeat them in the shower, or while exercising and tuning out your mom. The more often you repeat them, the better.

I personally like to repeat mantras when I'm feeling most insecure. While dating, some of my baggage came from the department of believing I didn't deserve someone financially stable. I remember dating a guy who had a job, a bedroom outside his parents' garage, and the income for a fancy dinner, but I considered this a novelty. One night, I was getting ready for an expensive dinner with him and his well-to-do friends. I was weirdly nervous, given that I grew up with means, but somehow I never felt like I deserved it. Nonetheless, I knew financial stability was something I really wanted in my life, and this meant learning to feel comfortable around those who already had it.

Going on dates at swanky hotels or visiting luxury homes

became triggers for me. At the time, I was an editor for a luxury magazine, so I had nowhere to hide. Instead these moments of insecurity became the perfect time to repeat my mantras. I would repeat them in my head, over and over again: *I belong here. I am worthy of being with someone who is financially stable. I am abundant in all areas of my life.*

This got me through the uncomfortable feeling of believing I wasn't enough. I was training my mind to see abundance and believe that I deserved it. I found that coupling visuals with mantras made the process of changing beliefs even faster, which leads us to the next step in downloading our new beliefs: visualization.

2. Visualize What You Want to See

Remember as a kid when adults said daydreaming was silly? Well, forget you ever heard that. Daydreaming, also known as visualizing, preps our brain to believe our vision is possible.

If you grew up around men who constantly had affairs, you might have a hard time believing that there are honest and loyal men in the world. Unless we're the visionary type, our brains need a point of reference to believe in what we've never seen.

We can see in two ways: physically seeing, like watching yourself in the mirror, and seeing with the mind's eye. The mind's eye is what we use to daydream or visualize the story our best friend describes, in detail, about her weekend in Tulum. The mind's eye exists to visualize what we want to believe.

The brain doesn't need new beliefs to play out in reality—imagining is enough. Your reality could be having too few loyal men around, but believing means trusting one to appear. You have to start imagining these men exist; we do this by visualizing, formerly known as daydreaming.

When we daydream, we typically aren't prepared for the daydream. It just shows up. Visualizing is a pre-planned event—just like mantras, you can do it whenever and wherever, provided you're aware of your intentions.

A few months before I met my now-husband, I made a decision to find love. I stopped sabotaging myself and did the inner work necessary to meet my future partner. One of the exercises I did was visualization. Most mornings, I'd go for a jog around my neighborhood, running through the shopping district known for wedding dresses. There I would purposely stare at the wedding dress displays, imagining I was inside the store shopping for one of my own.

Fast forward about a year and a half: my then-fiance and I are considering songs to dance to at our wedding. We're a few years apart with different taste in music, but we have mutual love for Dave Matthews Band. He suggests we use the song

"You and Me," and I nod my head with a little smile; "You and Me" was on the playlist I listened to while running down that street full of wedding shops.

We aid the believing process by offering our minds new visuals. We visualize to prep our brains to believe something different. Our imagination convinces us that something could be real.

Each day, spend some alone time with your eyes closed, imagining your future partner. Do it while you're showering, working out, or even stuck in traffic—just make sure to keep your eyes open! In fact, moving your body during the exercise supercharges your efforts, due to the impact of movement on the brain. Imagine your new mantras coming to life, and go nuts with your visual! You don't need permission to day-dream about your future.

3. Feel What You Want to Feel

To seal the deal, we need to feel what we want for ourselves in the future. When we feel poorly, our thoughts turn negative before our feelings, not the other way around. Feelings start with thoughts that we happen to believe, so while a thought may come up, we must believe the thoughts in order to produce a charged feeling.

Our feelings are clues that tell us what we believe, but sometimes new beliefs don't stick. Our lack of experience means we cannot feel the attached feelings, so we must introduce them in mantra and visualization whenever possible. It may be hard to call up new feelings for the first time, so think of someone who has had that feeling, like a character on a TV show, and imagine you're that person. How would you feel?

Look out for examples of people in your life who possess this feeling. Can you borrow it? This is what the best actors do, feeling their lines as they go along. When we watch them, we believe they embody the emotional life of their character.

Even if it takes time, I want you to read those mantras and call in your feelings. When you're imagining your future partner during visualization, ask yourself, *How would this make me feel?*

Please take this work seriously—just like eating healthy, doing it now and then won't release your magic. Eating healthy is a lifestyle. Exercising your mind and monitoring your beliefs is part of that lifestyle, but it takes dedication to actually see results.

FORGET FAKE IT 'TILL YOU MAKE IT

Remember, *fake it 'till you make it* is a different process. This is about abolishing the lies you told yourself so often they became truths. The truth is that you *are* worthy. The truth is there's someone out there for you. The truth is you *are* loveable. The truth is that whatever you deserve will be made available to you soon.

I'm not handing you a magic potion; think of it as healing ointment. This is not about tricking yourself into believing something just to attract more. This is about bringing you back to a natural state of being and believing. You were created to believe in love, to be consumed regularly by loving beliefs, but somewhere along the line that all got confused. Others projected their own confusion onto you, and now you face a network of false beliefs that keep you from happiness. The phrases, feelings, and visions you're introducing into your psyche now make up your truth. You've returned to where you always intended to be.

Step Six:
FIND A DATE

Feeling lighter, perhaps more optimistic? Awesome, that's exactly what we need to attract new suitors. If we attract with our hearts and minds full of baggage, we get more of the same. The reason you did this work was to see something new, so get yourself out there and watch your hard work pay off.

If you did all the prior steps, you are completely ready to start looking for dates. What, you thought your future partner would knock on your door and ask you out? Maybe your Amazon Prime delivery guy is single and cute (a girl can dream, right)?

For the rest of us, we have to take steps towards meeting the right person. The first step is getting yourself some dates! I know that sentence made you want to vomit just a little. Hear me out. There are several ways to get dates. Dating apps are probably the most popular way to do so in 2018—if that doesn't feel right for you, no problem, you do not need to go about it that way. Otherwise, dating begins to feel like a drag and a job.

This is *your* dating experience. If you like meeting people by chance, make sure you go out quite often. If you'd rather meet people through friends, let everyone know you're game for blind dates. If you like online dating then start making those profiles.

My client Sienna was in her 50s. She'd tried online dating but only met creepers. She didn't want to do it anymore. On the other hand, she really wanted to meet someone, feeling otherwise trapped that online dating was the only way to find that person.

Rather than quit, she decided to try a new strategy: dating through referrals. This felt good to her, so she asked everyone to set her up on dates. When she received an email from a childhood friend from summer camp, who she hadn't heard from in years, she asked her friend, *By the way, do you know anyone who you can set me up with?*

I was impressed, knowing that I couldn't be so vulnerable and make that kind of ask, but she had at least one date every single week, sometimes two, until the day she met her boyfriend. Referrals worked for Sienna, because that strategy made her feel safe. For others, asking for referrals might produce anxiety. You have to find the strategy that makes you feel good, otherwise you'll never get the results you want.

Many of us find dating exhausting because we play by rules that don't make sense. Let me tell you a little secret: there are no rules. All you need is to remember why you want this. That big picture vision gives you the motivation necessary to take small, actionable steps towards what you want.

Today, I want you to pick one strategy for making dates that doesn't feel icky. You may not be excited by any new strategies right now, but that's ok—pick one that doesn't make you vomit and go with it.

COOL GIRLS FINISH LAST

Now that you know which strategy feels good, you actually have to do it. Yes, *take action*. For those of us who fear looking pathetic, anti-feminist, or plain ole uncool, it can be uncomfortable admitting that we want committed relationships.

You don't need to go around telling everyone you're about to meet someone special, particularly if you're not going off referrals. But if someone were to ask, you shouldn't feel ashamed about admitting to your desires. Having shame around what you want sends out funky vibes, blocking you from the type of relationship you desire.

My client Carolina was dating pretty regularly. It was no secret that she wanted a boyfriend, except to the guys she was dating. Carolina had picked up the belief that being independent, cool, and desirable meant detaching from commitment. In other words, being too forward about her desires was unattractive and far from sexy. With this in mind, she found herself on date number six, with some guy with zero intentions of committing. She told herself, *I'm just having fun until the right guy shows up.*

With that statement alone, I saw that she had some faulty beliefs about dating. First off, she'd implied that commitment could not be fun, a belief held by so many people. While commitment could feel like throwing in the proverbial towel, if that were the case, why would fun-loving, adventurous ladies like us ever settle down?

The first step was redefining her idea of fun, getting clear on the pleasure she wanted for herself. For someone who just left a toxic eight-year relationship, a year of casual dating could be liberating, provided they approached dating with that self-awareness. Carolina was ready for something serious though. A bunch of short-lived relationships, although spontaneous and sexy, was not her idea of fun. She was denying herself commitment because she cared too much about her dates' opinions on her goals, and she continued to humor these ill-suited men.

After her first date with one guy, Carolina intuitively knew he wasn't ready for commitment, but she kept seeing him, hoping her intuition was wrong. She thought, *What's the harm? I don't have any other prospects at the moment, anyway.*

Six weeks into seeing each other, he broke things off with her because they wanted different things. If we don't end partnerships that ignore our truest desires, the universe does it for us. This hurts way more than doing it ourselves.

Carolina knew this wasn't going to work, yet she decided to ignore her intuition and continue the relationship past its expiration date. When he broke things off, she felt rejected with a bruised ego for not doing it first!

We can all sympathize with Carolina. She was exhausted and wanted this guy to be *the* guy, but fear of being judged prevented her from admitting she wanted commitment and led to her getting hurt. She fell in love with someone who wasn't available. When we search for dates, we must be honest with what we want. We must be clear about our intentions, though not necessarily with everyone—you don't need to write *Only looking for serious applicants* on your online dating profile.

You need to be clear with yourself. You must vow to honor your desires. This is how we show ourselves self-love, our souls forever whispering, *What you want matters, and I will do my best to honor that because I love you.*

One way to make good on our vows is with intentions. Each time you open that dating app and start swiping, set your intention. Setting intention is basically saying a prayer; it doesn't matter who or what you believe in, what matters is proclaiming your faith.

When you open a dating app or text that friend who promised to set you up—as you get dressed for that barbecue with friends—take a moment to set an intention like, *Please may I attract the loving relationship I seek.* Feel free to write it down. Grab your energy and give it a clear purpose, or else witness it run wild. You may be nervous, parts of you convinced the whole charade won't lead anywhere, but without setting intention, those toxic segments of your energy will come out and play.

HELP FROM ABOVE

Speaking of prayer, the spirit world has infinite assistance for you. Allow yourself to ask for help. I see this all the time in my practice; I've experienced overbearing, deceased grandmothers crossing over and playing unofficial matchmaker in heaven for their granddaughter. It makes me laugh and warms my heart.

In addition to past loved ones functioning as cheerleaders and fairy godmothers, we have spirit guides. You may have one working for you already, but if not, ask one to help you out. We have freewill, so our spirit guides need permission to step in. Then we must follow their guidance.

Understand you are not alone in this process. When desires are strong, they belong to our soul's contract. You've heard your soul's calling; now it's time to put in the work. We're sent to Earth with an army of heavenly assistance. The job of your guide is to make sure you fulfill your purpose, so if having a partnership is important to you, your guide will support you every step of the way.

MAKE IT A PARTY

Feeling alone is half the reason dating feels awful, but our loved ones want us to be happy, even if their delivery is flawed. You know those family members who ask, at every holiday gathering, "So my love, why aren't you dating anyone?" My mom loved to ask that kind of question, and I would respond, "Mom, seriously, do you think I want to be single? Do you know of any place where I can buy an eligible bachelor?"

Jokes aside, there are people in our lives cheering us on, so why not involve them and make the process more fun? We don't need to search through the apps, alone in our bedrooms, listening to "All by Myself" by Celine Dion.

My client Maria was open to dating apps, but she felt awkward using them. To lessen the pressure, she had some of her closest friends help her date online. She had wine, food, music, and lots of laughs—not only was she celebrating herself, she got stuff done!

Her best friend's husband took charge of swiping. He grabbed her phone, began reading profiles out loud, and consulted with guests re: making a move on her behalf. He ultimately found a guy who attended his high school and remembered as a really nice dude. He reached out as Maria and today those two are married. True story.

If we have fun in the process, we get more positive results. We come from a place of joy and abundance rather than fear. It's the difference between, *I need to do this* and *I want to do this.* When you're at a bar, dare yourself to talk to people you wouldn't. If you're working on referrals, entice your friend's competitive side by offering prizes, and remember that profile-swiping always pairs well with wine and friends.

THE EYE OF THE TIGER

It's up to us to make this process playful, but having fun doesn't mean not taking dating seriously. Remember, this is a strong desire to which your soul is calling. You must listen and act. When we ignore our soul's calling, we remove ourselves from our true path. Like any goal, we start motivated and excited to try new practices, but as time passes, the lack of desired results sends us off track. We need to remember that our results align completely with the effort we put forward.

When I say effort, I don't mean the masculine kind that involves constant doing and pushing. I mean waking up every day and working on yourself, keeping clean beliefs that manifest into action. If we only work when feeling pain over what we want, we never achieve lasting results.

What you do this month for yourself—setting dates, manifesting mantras, pursuing self-care— directly affects what you see in the coming weeks. Once you stop these efforts, the future weeks turn quiet, without much movement in the love department.

Keep the momentum going with reminders. Since you're a spiritual girl, you've probably heard of a vision board. If not, let me tell you how it works. A vision board is a collage of images that creates a visual representation of your desire. Once completed, you place the board somewhere where you see it every day. This gives us time to identify desires and how they appear, giving the brain examples of what to look for around our new goals.

I can testify to the effectiveness of a vision board. When I was single, I cut out pictures from magazines featuring happy couples in wedding dresses. I glued them to a small board and hoped to put them on display, but not too out in the open. I had two roommates; our house was typically the meeting spot for all of our friends, and I wanted to avoid total embarrassment.

I came up with the brilliant idea of hiding it inside my bathroom medicine cabinet, which now resembled the inside of a teenager's locker. When I reached for my toothbrush every morning, I was reminded of my goals. I figured no one would go in there.

Until the day my ex-boyfriend slept over.

I'd had a moment of weakness and found myself waking up next to my ex. That morning, he went looking for mouthwash and there was my vision board in all its cheesy glory.

Needless to say, we definitely stopped seeing each other afterwards. Let's just say we wanted different things, but that official split created the space I needed to meet my person. The vision board wouldn't let me forget about my intentions.

How many times do we decide we want something, work at it a while, and then forget about it completely? It's easy to forget because it's not a habit and there's no reminder. Everything we have accomplished in the past is because we've worked hard or thought about it positively every day.

I know it may sound dry to think of your desires as goals, but they are. Manifesting them means making them a priority in your life. You have to remember to want your goals. You have to remind yourself that the manifesting, swiping, mantra-ing, positive attitude, and self-reflection do matter. These little actions create your life.

I used to speak to my client, Michelle, once a year. We didn't have recurring sessions; it just worked out that way. Every year, around the same time (typically, right before the holidays), Michelle and I would schedule a reading. Every year, we discussed the same thing: her plateau at work, her desire for love, lack of dates, her family, and so on. Each time we spoke, I channeled the same messages and advice for her life; it was totally "Groundhog Day."

A lot of people think booking a session with me means hearing a predetermined future. Michelle was no different. Every year she set up a session hoping I'd say her man was near—that finally this was the year, but I could never tell her that.

She was meant to have a romantic partner in life, but she had some work to accomplish first —like putting effort into dating! In my sessions, I see paths for people based on choices they've made or may make in the future. Our desires belong to fate, but because we have freewill, our choices determine whether we're on the right path. Just because something is meant for us, does not mean it's going to fall on our lap. We have to make the proper choices to get there.

Michelle wanted love so badly. She had so much to give, a beautiful person inside and out, but fear convinced her that this desire was not a big deal. She distracted herself with work, traveling, family drama, or the latest handbag. She didn't understand that she could have all those things *and* a fun dating life leading to the man of her dreams. Fear convinced her that she had *all* these things to do before actively dating: buy a home, reach a certain position at work, lose weight…the list went on.

Every session, she received specific guidance for getting what she wanted in life. Her guides showed her little tweaks she needed to make to walk her soul's path. She left our calls with clarity and motivation to create the life she wanted for herself.

Every year, we would speak and nothing would ever change. The messages were exactly the same, because she forgot to make her desire for partnership a priority. After a few weeks of trying, she became impatient, lost focus, and stopped altogether, so she continued to find herself in the same place: single and looking for another plus one.

When we make something a priority, we think about it every day. It becomes an obsession. However, we don't feel rainbows and butterflies about it every day. Writing this book is a priority for me, and many days it make me want to cry. Writing is hard, girl! Putting myself out there, digging inside, staying focused…It's all challenging, but I know sharing this with you is part of my soul's purpose. I cannot live one more year without this book coming to life.

You have to get there. You need your back up against the wall. Refuse to let another year of unhappiness go by because you can't figure out this relationship thing.

I get that this process is excruciating. The reason it feels that way is because we're chasing demons from their hiding places. When we try to change, we go against some of our densest beliefs and fears. Identity and ego are tied to these insecurities of ours; going against them feels like the heart plummeting to the floor, as the body begins to crumble.

I understand it's not easy, but we are strong. We've all done something impossible at one time, creating a new future of possibility for ourselves in the process. You can do it again. You can and you will, but you must make it a priority.

FOLLOW THE SIGNS

When we commit to our desires and make them a priority, something cool happens: the universe conspires with us. If today, you fully commit to your desires and take action—even if you're afraid—the universe will organize itself to meet your desires. If you look for examples of this happening, you'll train your mind to see the abundance of life, and the more we look for abundance, the more it comes.

After you've made the commitment to go after what you want, look around for the signs that prove your work is actually manifesting. By doing this, you find that your intentions and prayers are being answered. You begin to realize you're not alone in this process. The universe and your guides are there waiting to help out and now that you've invited them inside, they can release their magic.

Imagine you're running a marathon. As you run through the course, growing weak in the knees, people cheer you on and hand you water from the sides. They are signs to keep going; they are so sure you can do this.

By looking for signs that show you what's working, you acknowledge the cheerleaders in the marathon of life. They give you the stamina to keep going; they serve as trail-markers in the greatest race of all time.

Your ability to see signs relies on understanding your intuition. Intuition is your biggest ally when it comes to dating. We're going to talk about intuition in every stage of the process, but for now, let's focus on using intuition to attract more dates.

We all have intuition, the ability to know something without conscious reasoning, yet we tend to favor logic over intuition. This becomes a problem because dating is a matter of the heart. We know this very well, but still we try to figure it out with our minds.

The mind is an incredible tool, obviously. It can make all sorts of realities. It can also create fear. If we rely solely on logic to get through this dating thing, we're going to run into fear, but if we spend more time in our hearts, where intuition resides, we'll understand that fear is not real.

After spending a lot of time in our minds, using intuition can feel foreign. It's not because you're bad at intuition, you just haven't used the muscle as much. Building up that intuition muscle is a worthy investment, because intuition empowers you to spot the good from the "total waste of time."

3 WAYS TO ACCESS OUR INTUITION

1. Feel Your Feelings

Intuition speaks to us through feelings. Unfortunately, we're not always taught how to understand feelings. In my practice, I find that most people understand what we feel on the superficial level, but women, in particular, have several layers of feelings. When a woman talks about her feelings at the basic level, she's often very far from the truth.

Men, on the other hand, have just a few layers. For this reason, we often find men frustrated with us because we don't say what we mean. They just don't always understand our complexity, because they're not built that way, but once they feel safe to share their own feelings, they're usually not too far from the truth.

Regardless of our gender, emotional awareness is the clue to uncertainty. Earlier in this chapter, we spoke about adopting the dating strategy that *felt* the best for us. After all, if the process doesn't feel right, we're not going to get the desired results.

It may seem like personal preference; someone may feel good about dating apps, while the other feels good about referrals. The point is, our intuition shows us the way. It tells us to follow that feel-good feeling, because in the end, what else do we want from relationships? It only makes sense to use a feel-good action to find another feel-good feeling, right?

On days where I can't get into my feelings, because I'm so in my head, I like to do a simple exercise. First, I place my hand on my heart and close my eyes, imagining my focus of energy leaving my mind and traveling to my heart. For a while, I sit there trying to connect to my heart. I take deep breaths in and out, and while I don't always *feel* right away, the exercise is not about finding an answer. It's about checking-in and cuddling up with my own heart.

Sometimes feeling our feelings can be hard, because we don't want to go there. For those of us who've buried our feelings for long enough, going there may feel like losing control. But until we allow our feelings to be felt, we are controlled by their shadow, working our entire lives around not confronting our own pain. When at the mercy of the shadow feelings, we're never truly in control.

At first, working with feelings may feel weird or uncomfortable, but that doesn't mean we should run away or stop doing it. Keep going—eventually it becomes the new norm. Besides, getting comfortable is a worthy investment when you find clarity in the process.

2. Be Present

Another way we converse with intuition is through being present. It's about stepping out of our own minds, removing ourselves from the constant internal dialogue. Imagine a person who doesn't stop talking. If that person speaks for ten minutes straight, chances are they're not going to hear or see anything else in the room but their own voice.

The answers to our challenges are not in the dialogue of our minds. The answers are always in the spaces we create while present. When we quiet our minds, the voice of intuition is heard. That voice will guide you, so give it some space to speak.

On a day-to-day basis, being present is about bringing focus to what's happening. We don't always realize it, but we spend most of our time considering the past or worried about the future. Rarely do we fully experience the present moment. When we hear about being present, it can sometimes feel like turning on an invisible light switch, but presence is found by engaging with the senses—any five of them will get us there.

On our honeymoon, my husband and I took a long bus ride to some ancient ruins. The drive was a bit boring. There was no television, no wifi, and my husband was asleep. My mind quickly drifted off to work, thinking about the articles I needed to write, the photo-shoots I needed to schedule.

All of a sudden, I caught myself; there was no way I'd think about work on my honeymoon. It was upsetting that work had trespassed on my consciousness. It's funny how we spend all this time planning out trips and barely stay present once we get there.

Determined not to miss my honeymoon, I decided to engage my senses. I first started with sight. I looked at the landscape, the people on the bus, the color of the sky, etc. I could tell you exactly what everything looked like that day, because I was truly there—no photos, no music, no distractions.

Pick one of your senses and try to focus on using it alone. For example, pick sound; close your eyes and notice what you hear. It's amazing what you'll find.

I did this once for a group of employees at their company office. After the exercise, the boss said, "We really have to change that light, because the buzzing sound is intolerable." Even though he was in the office every day, he'd never noticed the sound until that moment.

Whether we like it or not, setting up dates is part of finding love. There are so many different ways to get there. Rather than becoming overwhelmed or stuck in maladaptive patterns, count on your own inner guidance to tell you what steps to take on the path to love and commitment.

3. Tracking

While there are similarities between the nature of our intuition, it manifests itself in a variety of ways. For this reason, we really need to pay attention to how intuition shows up in our own lives.

You have to play around with this. If you feel something that may be intuition, make a note. Some people get goosebumps or strange sensations in their bodies. I often receive messages through other people, whether in-person, books, podcasts, shows—virtually anything. When this happens, I hear sounds louder than most of the conversation, as if someone dialed up the volume on one phrase within an entire paragraph. When dating, we may hear something the other person says very strongly. This could be a red flag or just a meaningful sign.

I also see images in my mind's eye, which feels like dreaming with your eyes open. A lot of people pass these visuals off as daydreaming, but if you pay attention, they often form messages or premonitions.

A lot of people describe their intuition as a feeling. The statement usually starts off with, *I don't know why I feel this way, but I just know…* That's the sixth sense we hear about sometimes, and we should never doubt it.

Seriously, never doubt it. For those of us who have been in abusive relationships—emotionally abusive counts the same—the worst damage is the loss of our intuition. People tell us that we're crazy or our feelings are unwarranted. We hear them speaking, but our body is telling us something else. As women, intuition is our strongest power. It's how we tell truth from lies. For this reason, people have been trying to strip us of it for centuries. We cannot allow this anymore.

Tracking our intuition is a process that leads us to trust ourselves. As we track, we get to know who we are and how we function. When we see the patterns of our intuition, we must guard them. The more you stand up for your intuition, the stronger it becomes and the less you doubt yourself.

Lastly, dreams are how guides and ancestors communicate with us. Of course, sometimes they're simply a manifestation of inner anxieties, but oftentimes they're much more. If you feel called to interpret a dream, go for it.

TEXT THIS WAY

Intuition is your best bud during the dating process. She's there to help in moments that make our stomachs turn, like texting.

We can't talk about setting a date without talking about texting. Regardless of your personal opinions on the subject of texting, it's a necessary evil. Lots of us want to focus on the good 'ole days when people chatted on the phone, but where does that get us? The first honest step to getting better at texting is accepting its role in this process.

I'd love to give you a formula to create perfect texts, but we know that's impossible. Every conversation is different and we need to depend on intuition to know how to write back. But there is one truth I want you to remember when texting: if you know deep in your heart that no matter what, you'll find a loving partnership, sending a wrong text will not sabotage that reality.

Some experts might encourage self-confidence with texting, but to me that's like saying, "All you need to do is buy yourself a magical unicorn." Instead, I want you to have faith in your vision.

If you remind yourself while texting that this dating thing is working out for you, you'll be less afraid of who is on the other side, or about writing the wrong sentence. The person you're texting isn't better than you. They're not smarter than you. They're just another human created by the same source that created you.

We often turn these potential dates into superhumans in our heads. It's like interviewing for a job we really want but may not deserve. We second-guess those texts, wondering if they're judging what we said. Sure, some people are going to judge our text messages, but do we want to be with someone like that? If the person on the other end is judging us, that's really not our concern. You can count on the universe protecting you by matching your energy. The judgmental person goes away on their own, as long as we don't judge ourselves.

On the flipside, when texting back and forth, we may think we're better than the other person. In this moment, we think we're standing in our worth. We think we're more evolved. But really, this is just the ego disguising itself to appear of higher caliber than basic fear. Both sides of the spectrum lead to the same fear: this is never going to happen for me.

If we approach texting as a tool for getting what we want, we breathe a sigh of relief. Text whatever feels good for you, and you can't mess this up! More than words on the screen, the person feels your energy; feel good about texting, and the other person feels that too. It may even lead to a first date, which by the way is our next chapter.

Step Seven:
DATING AROUND

A lot of people hate first dates, but I always loved them. I found them kind of magical. Laugh all you want, but think about it. In this world, we're so afraid of strangers. We feel so separate from those we haven't met, but dating means sitting down with a total stranger and hoping to sow intimacy. In our own little way, we're bringing the world together by dating.

Plus, there's so much hope in dating. Even for the jaded, the act of dating proves we believe. I know not everyone is looking for real love—come on, I'm not that much of an idealist, but even if you just want a hot bod in your bed, have hope!

There are endless surprises in dating. For better or for worse, dating gives our lives variety. One day, you'll be all coupled up, complaining about the tedium of monogamy. You'll think of me then; you'll look back and laugh at the time someone drank eight highballs and threw up all over your dress (or whatever happened to you).

Alright, I'll get off my soapbox now, but going on dates is supposed to be fun. When it doesn't feel fun, we're usually going about it all wrong. In this chapter, we're going to learn how to enjoy dating to the fullest.

A FRESH PERSPECTIVE

You've probably been on dates before, giving you unique thoughts about the process. Today, I'm asking you to forget it all. Pretend you've never been on a date before; you've only heard about how awesome they are. Since you've heard so many great things about going on dates, you're excited.

I know this can be a stretch for many of us, especially if we've been in the game a while. After so many unsuccessful dates, it's easy to feel disappointed. I get it. However, this slew of dates is different because of the work you did in the last chapters. Throughout those steps, you shifted and changed your future.

If it's hard to be optimistic about dating, ask yourself what's the worst that could happen. Your answer will probably have something to do with disappointment and rejection. This is very common. We often don't want to get excited because we're afraid of feeling disappointed. We keep our expectations low to manage the possibility of heartbreak later on. We come with this Debbie Downer vibe and wonder why it doesn't work out.

Guess what? Rejection is not scary because in the next chapter, I'm going to show you how to overcome it altogether, freeing you to date with an open heart.

Going on a date takes courage, and stepping into courage means remembering these two truths: 1) No matter what happens during and after the date, you'll soon meet your person, 2) No matter what happens during and after the date, you'll know how to handle it.

The first truth reminds us to have faith, believing our desires will come true. It insists we remember our soul's calling, meaning that true love will find us. We just have to do all the baggage-clearing work and be open to love.

The second truth reminds us to believe in ourselves and our intuition. We are asked to acknowledge and honor our strength, remembering the hardships we've overcome in the past.

DATING RESPONSIBLY

As I mentioned earlier, we hope to approach dating with an open heart, but there's a way to do this responsibly. When dating, our expectations tend to occupy one end of the spectrum; we either keep them low to protect our hearts, or we lay everything on the table and force intimacy. She who dates boldly appears courageous to some, but to others she's downright reckless.

Before each date, we set unconscious expectations in our head. We typically skew negative or overly positive in our thinking. When we tire of dating, we deal with exhaustion in two ways: proving to ourselves that giving up is the answer, or trying to make the next possible relationship stick.

Those who give up are driven by past experiences. We approach dating with our baggage from the last few loves or encounters. We believe that everything going forward will happen the same way. We project our feelings and punish the new date for what the last one did.

My client Chris was a dating machine. He really wanted to fall in love. The reason he wasn't in love was not because of a lack of effort on his part. He would go on date after date, and he expected I'd give him tips on how to be successful on first dates. Instead, I told him to stop going on dates.

Like many of us, he thought it was a numbers game—date as much as you can and eventually you'll find someone, but in fact, dating is about working through emotional blocks. It's doing so that leads us to the right person. Without doing the work, the right person will never find us.

Chris' block? He was very resentful, expecting to meet a girl who'd disappoint him somehow. It didn't matter if it were Mother Teresa, he'd be convinced she'd ghost him. No matter who he dated, the poor girl would not have a chance, always punished for the last gal.

Explaining this to Chris spawned a major shift. He could not believe he was doing this, seeing how unfair it was to everyone involved. Once he decided to leave the past in the past, guaranteeing every date a clean slate, he eventually met his wife.

While some of us approach dating with a negative outlook, others want to make things work at all costs. Of course, I believe in being optimistic, but not at the expense of missing red flags and being wilfully ignorant. For those of us who swing to this side of the pendulum, we typically don't see the damaging effects right away, but we'll talk about that in just a bit.

I bring this up because I want you to be efficient and effective on your dates. I don't want you to date around if you don't want to, because it can be a real grind and bring our spirits down.

We need to go on each date with a clear head. We need to give each person a clean slate. It's only fair—both for them and ourselves. If we go in with past baggage or a future agenda, we've wasted time and made things harder for ourselves.

Before each date, say a prayer. Ask that you arrive with a fresh mind, unbothered by the past or future. Give your date a clean slate and pray they return the favor. Be aware of your feelings and true to them, too, because it's not just a date. This is your life.

A PRAYER FOR FIRST DATES

May I see what is true

May I feel what is real

May I create space
for laughter, truth, and love

I am safe

I am protected

I am enough

YOU ARE HERE

Our biggest fear when it comes to dating is often disappointment. We go on four dates with someone; it seems to be going well when all of a sudden things falls apart. We're back to square one.

The pain of getting our hopes up is precisely what we try to avoid. The potential for suffering is why we avoid dating, but what if you dramatically lessened your chances for feeling this pain? I promise it doesn't involve self-medicating, either. If I could only offer one tip for dating, I would tell you this: be present on the date. What do I mean? Really be there, and I don't just mean physically.

You see, we typically bring our bodies and leave our minds somewhere else. For this reason, we either miss the magic or the red flags. Three months later, we learn that this person we've been with is a big fat liar, beating ourselves up for not spotting it sooner. Well, my friend, they probably showed you a long time ago they were a liar. You just weren't present to see it.

My favorite pastime on dates is matching my first name with their last name—very feminist of me, I know. The guy could have been telling a story about how he ran over his dog and kept driving on the way to meet me, but I was too busy monogramming towels in my head. A red flag completely missed.

Then there's those who judge in our head. My husband and I were on a double date once after fixing up two of our friends. The guy was telling a really fascinating story about his undercover detective work, and I could tell how passionate he was about it. He was doing his job for the right reasons.

At some point in the evening, my friend and I headed to the bathroom to chat about the state of the date. I mentioned that I found him passionate based on his story, to which my friend responded, "All I know is that somewhere in that story he mentioned shopping at JCPenney. That's where he lost me."

I burst into laughter, because women love to do this. I remembered doing something similar. I was on date number three with my husband; he looked at the menu and couldn't understand tuna tartare. *What kind of a person doesn't know about tuna tartare?* I thought. Throughout dinner, I let myself get distracted thinking he wasn't sophisticated enough for me. Obviously, I eventually got over myself and realized he was a keeper.

Funny enough, I wasn't the only one who (almost) missed out on my husband, simply due to empty judgments. At a party one day, one of my husband's friends came up and said to me, "You see that girl over there? She went on a few dates with your husband but thought he was weird for having a motorcycle and wrote him off. Tonight, she saw you two together and told me she judged him too soon."

Her loss was my gain. As for the motorcycles, he sold them after we got married. He found them too dangerous, and suddenly he had a reason to be safe.

We miss so much being in our heads on dates. Not only do we miss seeing the person for who they really are, but we also miss out on showing up as our most authentic selves.

If not judging or dreaming about our date, we're judging ourselves. *Am I talking too much? Did he look at me weird? Do I have something in my teeth.* The list goes on.

When we're present, all those worries go away. We become two equal people having an experience together. He's getting to know you; you're getting to know him. All you can be is yourself. Anything else would be starting off a relationship with a lie.

The other advantage to being present is enjoyment, because being consumed by thoughts is hardly pleasant. Even if we don't like the person, our experience is more enjoyable when we're honestly there participating.

When we're fully present on a date, a few things happen. First, we listen to the words. Listening with presence is a little different than how we may be used to listening. Typically we listen and comment or give an opinion after every sentence. This dialogue is happening in our head. When we do this, we skew our experience. We experience our opinions about the conversation rather than the truth of it. If we're present, what we do is observe. Thoughts may come in, but they're observations and not judgements.

Observations are important because they allow us to find clarity. How many times do you end a date and wonder how you feel about the person? Maybe you convinced yourself that you liked the person and then, a few dates later, realized he was totally not the one. This happens because we're not present and paying attention to our observations. Our observations let us know how we feel. They are intuitive hits that guide us towards the right path.

Without good observation skills, we immediately start doubting ourselves. Have you ever questioned your ability to choose a partner? You may feel that way after falling for lackluster guys who initially seemed great. If this becomes a pattern, you might doubt your ability to see the red flags when necessary.

Now that you are working on observation skills, you no longer need to be afraid of yourself. Observation coupled with patience and faith leads you to that person you imagined creating with your list in step three.

SLOW AND STEADY WINS THE RACE

Speaking of patience, you need it. I know you're exhausted. I completely get it, but you're about to find someone who's there for the long haul. This person holds a very important position in your life. Even if only for a few years, they undoubtedly impact your course of life. Whoever holds this role in our lives affects our careers, where we live, our health, our money, and so much more. For those of us thinking of having children, this person also influences how our kids grow up—so yeah, it's not worth the rush.

So often we convince ourselves that we like someone, just to stop this whole dating thing. I know I did, but that kind of pretending doesn't work when committed to a soul-led life. I know you want a partner, but you must stay true to your soul's desires. These aspirations need not be exclusive.

Sometimes we fall hard for the person, despite the red flags. We date people who don't match our list. We date them but don't speak up about our needs. Resentment and anger leech out of our relationship, and it's too late. The whole cycle starts again, as we find ourselves back exactly where we started.

My client, Katie, notoriously fell for men with untapped potential. She had this beautiful gift of seeing the best in everyone. She would date guys who were good people but didn't have their lives together, growing confused between her perception and reality of the guy. Inevitably, the relationships didn't work; her expectations were too far off the mark. She was not dating these men but rather their potential.

She did this for a couple of reasons. She thought she deserved a fixer upper, not a ready-made man, and ultimately had tired of dating. She wanted to move things along, so she sculpted her dates into something more, believing they'd praise the ground beneath her—unfortunately though, love doesn't work that way.

We women have a high tolerance for pain. We can hold our tongue for a freakishly long amount of time. We do this to be polite, believing that voicing our opinion isn't important, but with dating, this sets the tone for the relationship.

Let's say you go on a date and he suggests meeting at his place, rather than coming to you—because he's on your way. No big deal, right? It sounds logical, but let's say you want to feel feminine and cared for; it's on your list. Driving to pick him up doesn't align with your true desires. For fear of being a nag, you don't say anything. It seems like an isolated event, until you see the guy more often. Picking him up becomes the norm, and suddenly we're reminded of the small choices shaping our lives.

When we don't speak up about our needs, we make a choice. That choice leads to constantly picking up boyfriends on date nights. Having a boyfriend who doesn't pick us up becomes characteristic of our lives, simply due to the small choice of not communicating our needs. This is the power of choice; don't use it lightly.

Step Eight:
AFTER THE DATE

For some of us, going on dates is easy. It's the stuff that happens afterwards that trips us up. Unless the date was an obvious no, it's easy to get in our heads, especially during alone time, as we wait to interact with our potential mate again.

At some point, we're going to experience one of two possible outcomes, both revolving around rejection. Either we can experience rejection, or be the ones doing the rejecting.

Rejection can be really hard to swallow because it feels so personal. This is when narcissism comes out to play. When someone—a complete stranger most of the time—rejects us, we think there's something wrong with us. We don't feel good enough to be loved. When someone decides they don't want to move forward in love, we believe we're not pretty enough, skinny enough, interesting enough, the works.

Guess what? You are completely wrong. When a person rejects us, we see their preferences. If I'm wearing a pair of shoes you don't like, does that preference say more about you or me? When I hear that you don't like my shoes, I learn about you and your personal preferences; we are not learning about me. Just because you don't like my shoes, doesn't mean they're ugly. All it means is that you have another preference.

This is what happens when someone decides not to move forward with us in love. We may logically understand this, but somehow it hurts getting rejected. Why? Our minds trick us into believing that other people's opinions are more important than our own.

If I feel bad because you don't like my shoes, I'm empowering your opinion to become truth. I obviously bought those shoes because I liked them, and that's what matters.

Think about when you decide you don't want to move forward with someone. It's not personal. You don't think they're a horrible human being. For one reason or another, they don't give you the feelings you're after in relationships.

The idea is getting to the point where we can date and stand in our worth. Standing in our worth isn't about being blinded to our own shadows. It's not about thinking that we're right and everyone else is wrong. If we keep going on dates and get feedback that we're talking about our ex too much or being too negative, we have to eventually ask ourselves if there is any value for us in these statements. Someone who is able to courageously look at themselves, seeing the good and the bad, is someone standing in their worth.

Of course, we're human. We fall into doubt once in a while. We may even spiral into a place where dating doesn't feel safe. When that happens, hopefully we climb out of the darkness, but first we need tools.

That icky feeling of not being enough, because someone dumped us, means we must proactively remove ourselves from that energy. The longer we stay in that energy, the longer it takes to find our person. We need to know what practices bring us back to center. As soon as you see yourself in this dark place of doubt and fear, you must engage in those practices right away. One rejection can lead to years of fear and disappointment, if we're not proactive about returning to center. Here are my favorite tools for restoring our balance of energy.

5 WAYS TO COME OUT OF THE DARK

1. Music

One of the easiest ways to find our happy place is through uplifting music. I must admit, I love myself a sad song. I used to indulge in the darkest songs while dating, just to feel that emotion. I sought-out sadness because in some weird twisted way, I wanted to stay sad about my ex-boyfriend. The melancholy became a way of healing.

As I switched up my music though, I changed my energy. I pulled myself from sadness and into the future, simply by varying my tunes. If you find yourself in a perpetual state of doubt, fear, sadness, or any other yucky feeling, listen and watch your attention closely. If your playlists have a distinctly sad vibe, that's powerful—you may as well be surrounded by a bunch of negative friends.

I challenge you to seek out music that makes you happy. Play it in the car, while preparing meals, or to start your day. You will absorb the energy of the music. It is so powerful, yet so simple.

2. Movement

If you want to supercharge the power of music, add some movement. Remember the story I told you about running past the bridal stores? At that time, I was really trying to elevate my energy to attract what I wanted. Almost every morning, I went for a run with an uplifting playlist, almost guaranteeing myself a good day. My good days turned into good weeks and those turned into good months.

We have an energetic body, what is considered the aura. That energy gets stuck if we're not moving our body regularly. Sadness from an ex, unworthiness from mom, or fear of finances can all get stuck in our aura. It's normal to have those emotions and fears, but we must work to move them out regularly.

This is why exercise is so healing. Most of us exercise to lose weight, which can be one of its great benefits, but the real power in exercise is detoxing the body of stuck energy.

Movement detoxes and music both have the potential to uplift. When we add them together, we get rid of the old (movement) and introduce a new vibration (music). After feeling rejected, we bring in movement to expunge the energy of *I'm not good enough*, and replace it with *I am enough*, just by adding a song that supports that vibration.

3. Nature

One of the really cool things about being human is absorbing energy. Those of us who are extra sensitive may find this a curse, because we feel everyone's stuff and that can be overwhelming. Nonetheless, all we should look for is energy that matches the vibration of our desired feelings. Since we absorb energy in proximity to other beings, this means shifting our fate in relationships.

Everything has energy. Nature holds one of the sturdiest energies out there, and when I say nature, I'm not suggesting you visit Joshua Tree National Park. Nature is the grass in your backyard, the house plant in your kitchen, the sapling in your office lobby. All these things partake in Earth's natural cycles. If we set an intention to absorb this energy, we connect to our natural way of being. Nature reminds us that time is a factor in our growth. It reminds us that we need nutrients to thrive, and that we're part of a much bigger picture.

Those reminders are why staring at the ocean or hiking can be soothing. Nature grounds and reminds us of our power. When dating and feeling rejected, fear takes over and we forget about our potential. Fear disconnects us from the source, until we feel alone and stuck. Connecting to nature brings us back to a state of pure potential.

4. Reiki

When it comes to changing our energy, sometimes we need a little help. If we're still feeling confused about this process, Reiki can be a good option. A Reiki practitioner channels healing from their hands into your energetic body.

The practitioner helps to move out old, stuck energy from your aura. They also transfer healing energy for rest and repair. If you need some assistance learning to shift your energy, Reiki is a great option.

5. Journaling

Dating disappointments can trigger really negative thoughts. Those thoughts have energy. As we think about them, their energy gets stuck in our energetic bodies. This is how we fall into negative patterns.

For many of us, detoxing from that negativity means purging. In some instances, we can change our energy just by shifting with the exercises mentioned above. But other times, we need to release the toxins that are holding us back. For these instances, there's journaling.

Leave everything on the page. The feelings might not be pretty, but that's okay. They're better off on the page than within us. When we keep these thoughts and feelings in our heads, circling around like songbirds, they poison us. Journaling is an opportunity to surrender our worries to the light, allowing that energy to be repurposed through daily reflection.

The exercise is best done first thing in the morning. There's really no formula to it, but do your best not to control your writing. Your job means moving out of the way to let out those toxic feelings. Once you feel like your pages are starting to take a turn (this may take months), you can then start introducing new energy.

QUICK TURNAROUND

Our ability to process rejection has everything to do with our dating success. If we're not skilled at receiving the "bad news," if the relationship doesn't work out, it's easy to fall into a perpetual slump.

Often we date someone for a few months before it becomes serious, and then for one reason or another, it falls apart. Of course, we went into the relationship with the best intentions, so when it doesn't work out, we need time to build ourselves up again. Some of us stay in this purgatory longer than necessary, needing even more momentum to get back on the proverbial saddle. I'm not suggesting you avoid healing after a breakup—just don't take the rejection personal.

If we do, our down time fills with doubt about finding a partner.

We fall into a low. Eventually, we realize that not having a relationship is more painful than rejection. We convince ourselves to try again, but doing so means revving up our spirits. This takes time and effort, which ultimately delays the outcome. By shortening the time in between, we can be more efficient and protect our hearts in a healthy manner.

The truth is, very few of us are skilled in this area, because our logic tells us to look at the evidence. If these possibilities aren't blooming, obviously we're meant to be alone, right? When our dating efforts don't pan out, it's hard to believe anything else.

Luckily, our reality is often different from the truth. When a relationship does not flourish, it's nature's way of killing what won't survive the seasons of change. Instead of trusting this, we try to control the outcome, believing it should be something different. We blame ourselves or lose faith altogether, and this perspective begins a cycle of doubt that's hard to shake.

Instead, we want to learn to process rejection and endings in a healthy way. After we experience loss, we must give ourselves a reasonable time to heal, and then reinstate positivity to continue the journey we started.

We all become experts at rejection turnaround time by keeping the following principles in mind:

1. Become Unattached to the Outcome

The reason we become disappointed is because we create expectations around possible relationships. In other words, we became attached to the outcome. We attach ourselves to the outcome because somewhere within us, we believe our happiness depends on whether this particular relationship works out. We somehow believe this is our only shot at happiness. Of course, when it doesn't work out, we find ourselves lost.

To avoid this sudden drop, remember that your happiness doesn't depend on your relationship with this one person. You're seeking a loving relationship that adds to your personal fulfillment. You're not seeking one particular person. If they don't work out, that doesn't matter because your goals don't depend on one individual.

You are seeking a feeling, and there are many combinations to how it finds you, the combinations being possible partners. If this particular person doesn't work out, they simply weren't a vibrational match.

2. Remember the Truth

Detachment can sound heartless when it comes to dating, but it's not. We're able to detach from the outcome because we have complete faith in our ending. When we believe deeply that we will find our person, we don't see "rejection" as a step back. Instead it's evidence that we're getting closer, because we're out there trying.

This small switch in mindset gives us the stamina we need to bounce back from disappointment. The truth is, this is happening for you. We are capable of calling desires into our lives. Your desire means it's already real for you. Once you understand that, the vision you have for yourself appears in the universe. Your job is to align yourself with that truth.

3. Get Over Yourself

Again, rejection feels personal. It feels like a direct attack on our character. In our precious little minds, we think the person who ended things has dedicated time and energy to picking apart our idiosyncrasies. Now, isn't that a little narcissistic of us?

We can only see life through our own eyes. No matter how empathetic we can be, we're still experiencing life from our own perspective. What we forget is that everyone else is seeing life from their own lens as well; they're thinking about themselves and their own experience.

When someone decides they don't want to move forward with us, they're really not spending all this time thinking about us. They're just thinking about how this current situation doesn't align with their own desires. They're not necessarily aware of what they want. They just sense that *this* doesn't feel good. What they want may very well be zero commitment, so no wonder being with you doesn't feel good!

In the past, I had one of those ex-boyfriend relationships that continued well past the heart-wrenching break up. Of course,

I hoped that our casual, friendly dates would rekindle the flame.

After months of torturing myself with this situation, one day I finally asked about the pink elephant. "Are we ever getting back together?" to which he responded, "I just can't, my gut tells me it's not a good idea."

He didn't have a good answer for me. Looking back now, I understand. He couldn't put it into words, but what I wanted from a relationship was not what he wanted. We simply weren't a vibrational match. His decision did not make me broken or unworthy of love. It just meant that what I wanted—the needs on my list—were not things he could offer. He wasn't clouded with the desperation of deriving happiness from someone else; he was able to hear his intuition—his gut, and sooner than me. I am so thankful he did.

4. Get Honest

How often do we force relationships simply to end the pain of searching? We overlook red flags. We see what we want to see, yet our intuition whispers the truth: *This isn't the right guy for you.*

We keep trying and the craziest thing happens: he ends things first! Not only do we feel hurt but also ridiculous for not making the last move. We meant to do it but wanted to "see where things would go."

When a relationship doesn't work out, we have to be honest with ourselves. Did he *really* have everything on the list? Chances are we've stretched the truth, hoping this would be "The One."

If we look at the situation clearly, remembering old signs from our intuition, we begin to feel empowered. We knew this wouldn't work all along. Next time, we'll know how to proceed. Be thankful for this experience and remember what you learned for next time.

REJECTION AFTER SEX

Dealing with rejection after a couple dates is hurtful, but rejection after sex adds another layer of confusion.

To be clear, I do not feel sleeping around is a bad thing. We don't always need strong rules about when and how we get intimate with others.

When it comes to this topic, it's about knowing what we can and cannot handle emotionally. But the truth is, a lot of the time, we don't understand what's underneath the surface. Many of us think we have sex in an empowered way. We think we are in control, but as soon as they don't want to continue the relationship, we shrink.

Honestly, it's not our fault. The slut consciousness is so deep within us and our society, and depending on your cultural upbringing, you might feel it more. For many centuries, women have been taught to be ashamed of our sexuality, in order to stay in line with the patriarchy.

Sex, with the right intentions and within the right environment, can be beautiful, empowering, and fun. This doesn't need to happen exclusively within the walls of a committed relationship.

With that in mind, very few of us hold that level of confidence. Those who are immune to the guilt that comes with this behavior are very rare. It is not our fault. We are still healing as a whole.

The hope is that when we decide to sleep with someone who has not committed themselves to us just yet, we make this decision with very clear intentions. Often, we use sex as a tool for intimacy. Subconsciously, if we sleep with a man, we think we'll form a closeness that moves the relationship along. Sadly, many times, we feel it's something we must offer, often pressured to make the other person happy. Please, if you feel that pressure, love yourself and walk away.

If our choice to have sex is one that stems from fear, we undoubtedly feel used after learning they no longer want to continue the relationship. This is when sex complicates things. For this reason, people recommend that we wait.

But who are we kidding? Waiting is not always realistic. In an ideal world, we make the choice from a place of empowerment. We decide to say yes because we want to have fun. Perhaps we feel safe with the person and know they will remind us of how sexy we really are—sometimes, sexy sex is what we need to heal and feel empowered.

For all the other times, do not shame yourself. A quick change in perspective turns those hurt feelings around.

If this happens, examine why you attracted this person. What belief brought you to them and this moment? This situation is an opportunity to review your strategy, the "disappointment" answers your prayers if you let it.

My client, Alina, was recently divorced. Her marriage was so broken for a long time, she felt ready to date again just a few months after the split. Shortly thereafter, she met a charming guy who made her feel appreciated and desirable; the fling was a welcome surprise, so when the opportunity for intimacy presented itself, she accepted.

The day after they slept together, he began to distance himself. Naturally, she took his behavior personally, spiraling into a puddle of remorse.

She thought her choice to have sex stemmed from pure intentions. The truth is, she let her guard down because he made her feel good, especially in the moment. When things changed the next day, she felt used. Not only did he cease being attentive, he obviously didn't want to enjoy her company in public. She felt like a piece of meat.

When I asked her to think about why she attracted this person, I understood that she, too, didn't want a public relationship. She'd just gone through a divorce; Alina didn't want to be judged by others. Subconsciously, keeping any new relationship on the down-low seemed best at the time.

Additionally, she became aware of a repeating pattern in her life: her ex-husband and first boyfriend (post-divorce) both lived a double-life. Connecting these dots led her to an important epiphany, proving there is medicine in disappointment.

She felt icky when he changed after they slept together, but it wasn't for the reason she thought. The sensation of feeling used stemmed from not being a priority in this person's life. It wasn't the sex. It was the shame associated with the subconscious belief that she wasn't good enough to have someone who loved her unconditionally.

WHAT IF WE MESSED IT UP?

While we can intellectualize rejection and understand it's not us, but them, it still hurts. If we don't catch ourselves, it's easy to assume the blame for the demise of our relationship.

Maybe you went to bed with him too soon. Maybe you sent too many text messages. Maybe you had one too many drinks. Did any of these actions really derail you from finding the love of your life? Heck no.

What gets in the way of true love is obsessively replaying the past. We are, undoubtedly, going to trip and fall during this process, but just like a young child learning to walk, we get up again. The child doesn't judge herself for falling. She doesn't start criticizing herself for not getting it right. She intuitively understands that stumbling is part of the process of getting where she wants: in her case, to freedom.

Your desire for partnership needs to be stronger than your desire for perfection. If you care more about what people think than your desire to find love, then yes, rejection and these small missteps will hurt. They also continue to delay you.

But you can choose yourself first. You can love yourself so strongly that every time you slip up, rather than kick yourself down again, that voice in your head whispers, *That's okay. You're almost there. Keep going.*

This isn't another positive-thinking scheme, but encouragement. All of us were kids in the past. We can agree that encouragement is crucial to success. Whether we received it from the adults in our lives is irrelevant. We are now the adults, so be your own mother. Hold yourselves with care and be free to make mistakes.

This does not mean mantra-*ing* your way through disappointment, but being a compassionate mother. She ensures you have a community to pick you up when you fall down; she finds the right experts to complete the healing you are not able to do alone. She speaks words of love into your heart, like *You are not messing this up. Let's keep moving.*

WHEN IT'S A YES

Many first dates lead nowhere, but sometimes they surprise us. Here, two strangers decide to move forward in hopes of finding what they need, presenting the second possible outcome in love.

Rejection may be hard, but this part of the program is where my clients' anxiety hits an all-time high. The pressure is on, and we really don't want to make the wrong move.

The first truth to remember is that we're not the only one involved. As the budding relationship progresses, we are left to manage our own anxiety. Every reaction from the other person is meant to ease our personal anxiety, but unless we've mastered the art of detaching from outcome, we're going to expect that the other person's actions ease our nerves.

We judge every text message that he sends, or we fish for a reaction by initiating some sort of false connection. In other words, we focus on relieving our anxiety rather than being present for what is really happening.

When we've started to see someone pretty regularly, without commitment, it can feel like dating purgatory. All we sense is uncertainty. Naturally, we begin to go into survival mode.

In this emotional state, we forget there's another person involved. We see the situation with tunnel vision, only considering how we're personally affected—and yet, we're trying to form a relationship with another person.

At this time, it's important to understand our feelings. We're nervous about making a wrong move. We're nervous about the future and scared of opening our hearts. These are totally normal and expected feelings, but we don't want to drown in them.

We want to feel and acknowledge our feelings. Understand that our insecurities are being tested and may act themselves out. Our goal is not to rid ourselves of these feelings, but instead to work through feeling uncomfortable in the healthiest way possible.

Imagine you're exercising. There's a point where you make a choice to work through the pain or give up and walk out of class, like in yoga when you hold an uncomfortable position for an unreasonable amount of time. This is pretty much the moment we're looking at in dating.

We can hear the instructor yelling, *This is when change happens.* When the class finishes and we realize we didn't die, we think to ourselves, *That wasn't so bad.*

The same thing that gets us through those hard workouts can guide us through the uncomfortable feelings in dating. We practice deep breaths, we grab ahold of our thoughts, and we sink into the uncomfortable feeling until we become one with ourselves.

When comfortable with the uncomfortable, we're no longer enslaved by anxiety. Before reaching this point, everything we do is ruled by easing this pain, leading to all sorts of inauthentic decisions and living without alignment with who we want to become. Instead, we just show up as a ball of nerves. If we can understand what's happening in these moments, we can compassionately talk ourselves through the discomfort.

IT TAKES TWO

If we cannot acknowledge our fears by now, the most damaging result is forgetting about the other person. We may think we're focusing on them, because we're thinking about them all the time, but our thoughts revolve around their perception of us. That's not thinking about someone else. That's just thinking about us.

Why does this matter? What about all that talk about writing down what *we* need? We handle those things in the beginning to ensure we're in the right place before we start attracting. Whether we know it or not, we're calling in something.

Once we've called someone into our life, our creation is no longer in our heads, but physical form. Your partner is a living and breathing entity with a mind of his own. If we love our creation, we respect the ideas and desires it holds. This concept is synonymous with God's intention of giving us free will. This infinite source created us, but it also respects us. When we are creating, we need to do the same.

When we recognize the relationship is not only about us, we become present. Our intuition turns on. We see the other person as an equal, rather than some demigod holding the keys to our future. All of a sudden, they come down from the pedestal we've created.

After dating enough guys, I realized they were my equals. What a realization! I didn't think I was better than them, I just started to understand that they were humans full of insecurities and baggage, just like me. This was a game-changer across the board.

I once dated a particularly kind soul. I was fully present outside my anxiety, so I automatically saw him. We'd sit together amongst his friends, and I observed the manner of his behavior, noticing how he was different from the others. I could tell that he longed to be understood.

I could recognize this in him, because I had that in me, as well. This is how we connected. Ultimately, we didn't move forward because we couldn't negotiate our different cultural obligations, but the connection we had for that brief time was real and very sweet.

The truth is, we all want to be seen. If we can offer that to someone, even just for a short amount of time, we create space for healing, which is one of the greatest gifts we give. You may think to yourself, *of course I'm able to do that; I'm intuitive*. I will remind you that we're *all* intuitive. Sometimes we just need more practice.

Honing our intuitive skills starts with listening. That's all I did for this guy. I listened to him with an open heart. My priority wasn't to lock down a boyfriend, but connect to people by truly listening. This is our way of saying, *I see you*.

I was once on a plane to Las Vegas for a bachelorette party. All my girlfriends were in two rows, but somehow I ended up three rows back, in the swarm of Vegas partiers. I was thinking how nice it was to take a break from being a mom to two young children, and these guys were throwing back shots with breakfast.

As time passed, I realized they were exactly what I needed to brush off my overly nervous, uptight energy. We shared stories, and I learned one was a high-producing sales person for a luxury brand, while the other ran a family-owned sneaker store in Miami. Then I told them about my writing career. By the time I was wrapping up my story, the sales guy turned to me and send, "Wow, you're very accomplished. You must be proud," which made me understand that he was listening. He gave me a platform to be me. He understood that I was talking about my career because I was proud of my accomplishments.

I turned to him and said, "Now I see how you sell so well. You make all these women who come into your store feel good by making them feel heard." He affirmed with a wink. Of course, this guy was using his powers of listening and intuition to make a good commission. He made people vulnerable just by offering them an ear; he made them safe by giving them space to be themselves. Now he was off to Vegas, dropping crazy cash all because he was a damn good listener.

Listening is not only an amazing gift, it helps to avoid being consumed by our own anxiety. Good listening requires presence and focus. When present, we limit the access of fear-based feelings. Worry, doubt, jealousy, and other ego fears can't penetrate our energy when we focus on listening.

When face-to-face with someone, listening is an obvious tool, but we should also listen while texting. If *really* listening, we use our sense of hearing to understand what the person means, but we also use our intuition to sense energy. For those of us who feel being overly sensitive is a curse, now is the time to see it as a blessing.

When deciphering a text message, we need to activate our intuition. We don't have the benefit of body language or tone of voice. All we have are words on the screen. As someone who strings words together for a living, may I remind you how much wisdom there is in the words we use. As for emojis, you're on your own there.

There's a difference between overanalyzing and intuitively reading, so please proceed with caution. The trick to using intuition while texting means stepping out of our bodies. Usually, we read a text from our point-of-view. *How does this affect me? What does this mean about me?* These are the kind of questions we filter through the message.

If we read the text without an agenda, we pick up on what they're trying to say. In other words, if we decide not to take the text personally, we have a better understanding of what they mean. We gain energy by standing in our worth, and since feeling completely confident all the time is impossible, repeating the simple phrase, *If I were in my worth, how would this text make me feel?* often goes a long way.

If we feel our way through the text, there's a real opportunity to connect and let the person know we see them. We don't do this to manipulate, like the sales guy. We do it because connection is why we date in the first place. This is all about being authentic.

In addition to the gift of connection, now we also have the ability to avoid red flags. No matter how many great tips people give you on proper texting techniques, you're all alone with that response. The best thing to do is trust your intuition.

There are times when fear disguises itself as intuition, but we tell the difference depending on how it personally feels. If you feel attacked, that's a sign your antenna is a little off. If you're not sure, go back to the intuition-building tips mentioned in the previous chapter.

CONTROL ISSUES

Sometimes we freak out during the purgatory stage of dating, because we're afraid of losing control. Our future can shift without our say; our hearts may open without permission, and our imperfect selves risk being seen.

First, we are faced with our need to know everything. For better or for worse, we need to embrace mystery now more than ever. Two people are coming together and both need to decide whether this relationship will continue. As you suspected, you don't have control.

If we fail to trust, we drive ourselves and our potential partner crazy. Thoughts of an unsure future create an anxious mind. In the courting phase, we want to shake off that anxiety and feel sexy in our worth.

In this phase, clients often ask if I can see their near future, but our future is not confirmed until we make decisions. During the courting phase, we observe and wait to see if commitment is in the cards. A conscious dater knows they need time to observe and feel around for the right choice. We can't rush this process along.

Some of us commit prematurely, becoming attached to the outcome and putting ourselves at a higher risk for getting hurt. We open our hearts too early, without enough information.

I don't suggest waiting around collecting data to analyze and eventually come to the right conclusion. As I mentioned, relationships are a matter of the heart, so we should be using that part of ourselves to make decisions. Although our feelings have incredible intelligence, they too need time.

If we don't feel overwhelmed by happiness after the first date, sometimes we assume the person isn't right for us. Other times, we feel completely taken aback by someone and convince ourselves he's the one. Both of these approaches try to control the outcome.

Between the first meeting and commitment, the best gift we give ourselves is staying connected to our feelings. We need to trust and respect our inner guidance system to show us the right path. This will feel unnatural because the anxiety of not knowing can take over. If anxiety does take over, our default mode is controlling the outcome in whatever way possible, in order to feel better quickly. However, if we just sink into that feeling, we find medicine there, too.

Often in life, we don't know what we're doing wrong. We don't understand why we keep hitting walls. When someone tells us to follow our heart, what we typically look for are the happy feelings. We think the heart is all about the gushy stuff. But it's not.

The heart is about truth. And sometimes the truth is we feel anxious because we want to control. We want to control because we're afraid of experiencing yet another disappointment. We're afraid of disappointment because we fear it means we are unlovable. We're afraid of being unlovable because we need connection to survive. If we don't have connection, we fear, well, dying.

That anxious feeling brings us to this truth. Maybe it's not the truth we're looking for, but it's still a worthy clue. In fact, it's *the* clue. The walls we hit are because of what's buried under the need to control. If we can find what's underneath, we can begin to heal and work from there.

Do we need to heal completely to feel confident dating? I don't think so, but it's important to know what we're up against. With this information, we can compassionately walk ourselves through the process.

When a loving mother sees a wound in her child, she does not demand that the wound be healed immediately. Instead, she is aware of the wound. When the child is most vulnerable to feeling it, she talks and loves the child through it. She is not able to do this until she is aware of the wound in the first place.

Our wounds show up where we need them the most. When they show themselves, we need to lovingly mother ourselves. We don't stop nor try to control the journey. We embrace and remind ourselves that it's going to be alright.

GETTING TO TRUST

One quality of the divine feminine is trust. When we're in our truest form as females, trust comes naturally. We trust that the universe will provide. This stems back to the times when we lived off the land. The land provided everything we needed. There was no reason to ever doubt that.

Our lack of trust in the universe may not have bothered us before, but when it comes to dating—especially in the courting stage—trust is essential to remaining aligned with our authentic self. Without trust, we become like a nervous ball of energy. We can't control our feelings or actions, and before we know it, we've sabotaged a potential good match.

These are the moments we feel like, *Maybe I messed this up*. We feel that way because we didn't show up as our true self. Our true self is poised. Our anxious self, drowning in fear, is not. Trust is our solution to not going down this path.

Not only do we trust to embody our authentic selves while dating, but also because there is a certain level of unique mystery to this process. Mystery, the unknown, is something always present in our lives. Many of us try to close our eyes to it, hoping that we can bypass the mystery by educating and preparing ourselves enough not to face it.

In dating there is an exceptionally high level of mystery, because we're calling a new person into our lives. They bring in their own universe, which we know nothing about. To find the person we're going to collide with, we have to meet so many other potentials. Every time we meet one, we can't help but peek into our future with this person. When we do this, we realize how much we don't know. And that often causes us to worry.

The only way to accept mystery and the unknown is to trust.

When we don't trust, we spend time worrying about the "how." We wonder, *How is this all going to work out?* We employ our minds to come up with a solution, but it can't. Because, news alert: we don't know everything. We don't know all the answers. There is so much mystery in this universe, and we are so far from understanding it all.

Instead, we trust. For a long time, I thought trusting was for simple-minded people. I thought if I studied and searched hard enough, I could find answers to life's mysteries. I would end up in these mind traps that made me feel insane and again more doubtful. I often wished I could be those people who belonged to those huge religions that blindly trusted. But that's just not how my mind works. It always wants to know more.

Then I learned that in order to get more information–to learn more about the how—you first have to trust. It's the best form of surrender. When we trust, we acknowledge that there is something bigger than just our human selves. This is great news, because we no longer need to control everything. Instead, we can allow something to take care of us. We can finally learn to receive.

Unfortunately, most of us have forgotten our innate ability to trust. Especially now that our roles have evolved, we've taken on a lot of masculine traits—push, logic, perseverance—and have forgotten the feminine ones. Some divine feminine traits are intuition, flow, the ability to create from nothing, the innate worthiness to receive, sensuality (yes, you can totally flirt), and trust.

The good news is that we just need a refresher course on how to use them again. We don't need to achieve the ability to trust. It's already programmed within us. Unfortunately, it's a rare occurrence to see women leaders exercise their feminine powers. Although this is changing, typically we see women in power using masculine traits.

In many ways, we are already trusting. Every night we go to sleep, we trust that the sun will rise in the morning and signal a new day. We trust that we'll find food for our next meal and shelter when we come home. No matter how jaded we may feel, we all have the ability to trust. In fact, each of us is actively trusting someone and something every day. We trick ourselves into believing that we are in control, but really, we rely on trust all day long.

Trust comes from a mixture of gratitude and expectancy. It starts with gratitude because when we start to become thankful for even the smallest things called into our lives, we're collecting evidence. When we try to rise from one way of thinking or being to the next level, we must present a solid case to our brain in order to convince it to change.

Gratitude is the prosecutor collecting all the proof that it is—in fact—safe to trust the universe. Why? Look at everything it brought us thus far—our home, our clothes, our pets, this book. Sure, we often feel like we bought or worked hard for these things ourselves. And yes, to a certain extent we did. But what really happened was we co-created.

We thought of something we needed or wanted. Once we believed it was possible, our thoughts started to attract those things. The universe provided by actually making those things physical, way before we even decided to want them.

When we see this pattern over and over again, we start to understand that, *Wow, the universe does provide.* Now that we know this, we can start expecting life to work that way forever. If it does not work that way, it means that something is seriously wrong. Because the universe is set up to provide us with what we believe.

Through gratitude, we discover this truth every time, therefore we can trust it will continue to work this way until the end of time.

Surrendering to mystery has its practical advantages, as well. When in a state of trust, we're free of fear. And when we're free of fear, we have the clarity to know what we need to do, as we wait to see if this relationship will be committed or not.

When we're faced with crafting the perfect text message or going on a first date, most of us won't have access to a dating expert whispering in our ears. We must depend upon ourselves, which is why all of this work is about making us stronger.

Honestly, this work is about bringing you back to you. It's about bringing you back to who you were before all the disappointments, before all the negative talk projected your way, before all the wounds.

Your truest self knows what to do. The work we just did together in this book was simply two people taking out the trash. We removed all the layers of junk that made you believe you were something less than a creation of the highest form of love.

You are completely capable of calling in what you want and need. All you have to learn is how to leave your baggage at the door.

Step Nine:
LIVE

You have just completed decades of work. Whether or not you're aware of it, the journey you just went through has healed both yourself and your ancestral lines. I bow to you with honor.

Thank you for doing this work. Thank you because you are now on track to finding the right relationship for *you*, one that assists your soul in expanding, which by default expands the rest of us. If you decide to have children, you will be a better parent because you are happy and supported. This matters not just to you, but to all of us.

The next question is: Now what?

The answer is, you don't sit and wait, but rather you live.

You have full permission to live. If finding the love of your life is all about raising your energetic vibration, the best thing to do right now is follow your happiness and intuition.

Buy the property. Travel the world. Wear the clothes. Eat the food. Flirt. Laugh. Cry. Turn your life upside down with the intention of being free.

Live.

Do not be mistaken. Following happiness and intuition is not always a pretty road. In fact, it may seem destructive. But know you are breaking down so that you can build up to your truest self.

Your partner wants to meet your truest self, and while it might be a while before you fully accept her, your partner will recognize that person if you show her off every so often.

You're doing this work for you. You're living this life for you. Attracting that sacred union is simply the inevitable cherry on top.

Continue to walk the path with focus and an open heart. Trust that what has been promised to you will be delivered soon.

With all my love,
Nikki

57744326R00083

Made in the USA
Columbia, SC
13 May 2019